1992

THE SEARCH FOR
SAINT THÉRÈSE

By the Same Author:

FICTION: *A Gentle Fury*
            Bold Encounter

NON-FICTION: *Conversation with Christ*
                 A Girl and Her Teens

THE SEARCH
FOR
SAINT THÉRÈSE

Peter-Thomas Rohrbach, O.C.D.

HANOVER HOUSE
A DIVISION OF DOUBLEDAY & COMPANY, INC.
GARDEN CITY, NEW YORK

Imprimi potest: Christopher Latimer, O.C.D.
Provincial

Nihil obstat: Edward J. Montano, S.T.D.
Censor Librorum

Imprimatur:✠ Francis Cardinal Spellman
Archbishop of New York

April 11, 1961

The excerpts from *Two Portraits of St. Thérèse of Lisieux* by Etienne Robo are used with the permission of The Newman Press; those from *The Hidden Face* by Ida Friederike Goerres with the permission of Pantheon Books, Inc.

Dedicated to the memory of my mother

CONTENTS

LIST OF ILLUSTRATIONS

INTRODUCTION

On a humid August afternoon in 1958, I was standing in front of the Carmelite convent at Lisieux. The Rue du Carmel was thick with people, some turning into the Carmelite chapel, others making their way toward the souvenir stores to pick and choose among the unbelievable pious bric-a-brac sold in this pilgrimage town. It was warm and noisy, and tinged with the unpalatable flavor of commercialism. There were only two souvenir stores on the street immediately in front of the Carmel, but around the corner on the main road up to the Basilica the stores stretched, side by side, for blocks. And the variety of possible purchases was astonishing: articles which had been stamped or imprinted with some representation of St. Thérèse—a kerchief, a letter opener, or even an ash tray with St. Thérèse smiling vacuously at you from the bottom of the dish.

Yet, despite the uncomfortable air of business and enterprise, Lisieux remained a place of pilgrimage in the truest sense of the word. Masses were attended all morning in the chapel and the Basilica; row after row of people received Communion; confessions were being heard continually; the chapel was filled and emptied a hundred times a day as people knelt to pray and invoke the help of the young saint who once lived in this town. And earlier that very afternoon I had attended a procession and Mass in the Basilica where over two thousand people chanted the *Salve Regina* in unison.

Standing beside me surveying the jostling crowds was a tall and dignified English priest, Msgr. Vernon Johnson. The Monsignor had first visited Lisieux some thirty-three years before as an Anglican clergyman traveling in France, and that visit witnessed his conversion to Catholicism. In the intervening years he had lectured and written about St. Thérèse, and each summer he leads a group of English pilgrims back to Lisieux. Now, his eyes squinted in the bright sun, he was discussing Lisieux with me. We talked of the huge crowds and the two thousand people in the Basilica that afternoon. He nodded his head softly, pointing down the busy street. "But none of it would have happened if a little fifteen-year-old girl hadn't walked down that street one day and into the Carmelite convent."

And the Monsignor was right: all of it—the devotions, the crowds, even the artless souvenirs—derived from a young Norman girl, Thérèse Martin. It was an idyllic story of a sweet little girl who lived in Lisieux, entered the Carmelite convent, and died there at the age of twenty-four. Before she died she wrote her memoirs, a warm and personal account of her short life, and they were published after her death. "The whole world will love me," she said in the last year of her life, and it soon seemed to be true as her autobiography was translated all over the world and hundreds of thousands of pilgrims began to descend on Lisieux. This was the idyl.

However, about forty years ago some questions were raised suggesting that perhaps the story was not as simple and charming as we had first imagined, that possibly her rise to fame had not been as spontaneous as we were led to believe. More questions were raised, more studies undertaken, more evidence unearthed, and finally the stern accusation was issued that a gigantic pious fraud had been perpetrated at Lisieux, that the true image of the saint had been camouflaged under a coating of sentimental pietism.

The first rumblings of accusation were heard when it became known that St. Thérèse's autobiography had been thoroughly revised and corrected prior to its publication. Then it was discovered that the photographs released by the Carmel of Lisieux had been heavily retouched, making it almost impossible to ascertain the true likeness of St. Thérèse. This had all been done, the critics maintained, to present to the public an image consonant with what the Carmelite nuns thought was the traditional picture of sanctity. The manuscript, the photographs, the nuns' own recollections had been ruthlessly and irresponsibly edited, changed, and even deleted when necessary, so as to force the memory of the young nun into that preconceived and artificial concept. What we finally possessed, they claimed, was not a human, virile account of a young woman's growth in holiness, but only a sentimental fable; not an honest picture of a saint, but only a grotesque caricature.

The passage of time only seemed to reinforce the critics' position and add the mark of authenticity to their charges. New evidence was either discovered or revealed, new evidence which came in the nature of an exposé and seemed to cast dark and unfriendly shadows over the Carmel at Lisieux. Actual, unretouched photographs of St. Thérèse were produced and compared with the official photographs released by the convent; and it became distressingly clear that the retouched photographs

—the "faked photographs," as Etienne Robo calls them—
bore little resemblance to the original pictures: the honest,
forthright features of the young French girl had been
carefully obliterated and painted over so that there
remained only a rosy-cheeked, serene, rather insipid-
looking nun in the worst traditions of ecclesiastical art.
Then, in 1956, after a great deal of hesitancy and delay on
the part of the Carmel, the unedited version of St. Thérèse's
manuscript was finally released, and it seemed almost
incontrovertible that some kind of literary dishonesty had
been committed. The facsimile edition of the autobiography demonstrated that over seven thousand changes had
been made in the text before publication, that parts had
been erased and written over, that whole sections had
been deleted. In fact, almost one third of the whole text
had been cut before publication. This apparently was irrefutable evidence, so convincing that it seemed to close
the case. Thus, the British author, Lancelot Sheppard,
found himself driven to this uncomfortable conclusion:

> In 1953 M. Marcel More in a long article in *Dieu
> Vivant* . . . declared roundly that the whole tenor of
> St. Teresa's teaching had been falsified. Examination
> of the facsimile shows that the quotations given by
> M. More were accurate. . . .[1]

There has been some disagreement among the critics
themselves as to the amount of culpability which should
be assessed to the Carmel of Lisieux for foisting a fictitious
image of a saint on the world. Some of the indictments
suggest that there was some amount of active dishonesty
involved; such, for example, is the contention of Father
Etienne Robo, writing about Mother Agnes' editorial
work on the manuscript:

The purpose of Mother Agnes was edification rather than factual exactitude, and for this reason she did not scruple to leave out any incidents that might seem inconsistent with the conventional and popular idea of what a saint should be like.[2] . . . If her editing had gone no further, we could deplore her indiscreet zeal, but we should not be entitled to accuse her of distorting the truth.[3]

Other critics argue, though, that there was a more subtle, and perhaps more devious, construction of St. Thérèse's image by the omission of a detail here and the heavy underscoring of a detail there, so as to fabricate the desired result: this is the thesis of the challenging German authoress Ida Goerres, who claims:

The truth was never tampered with. . . . Nevertheless, a fabulous array of tiny accents, dabs of colour, lighting effects, remodelled and retouched the total picture so that it conformed perfectly to the current ideal. Even without these embellishments Thérèse fitted that ideal pretty well; as it was, the desired portrait and the reality were not only joined as closely as possible; they were completely fused. Thérèse became an angel in human form.[4]

But, whether the indictment be active dishonesty or careful rearrangement of the facts, we are left with the same unpleasant conclusion: we have been duped, we have not known St. Thérèse, we have had a false and misleading picture of a canonized saint.

This is a serious and disturbing charge, one worthy of our most careful and calm investigation. And that will be the task of this book—to examine the indictments, to attempt a discovery of the truth and the facts in the case, as objectively, as dispassionately, as logically as possible.

This is a formidable undertaking, yet one which is, I feel, of vital importance. We are dealing here with a canonized saint, someone proposed to us by the Church for our imitation and emulation, and as such, any saint deserves our most painstaking scrutiny and investigation. But there is even more at issue in the present case, I think. St. Thérèse and her doctrine have received an approbation and recommendation accorded to few other saints in the entire history of the Catholic Church. St. Pius X has called her, in a now-famous phrase, "the greatest saint of modern times." Pope Benedict XV said of her message: "There is a call to the faithful of every nation, no matter what may be their age, sex or state of life, to enter wholeheartedly upon this way which led Sister Thérèse of the Child Jesus to the summit of heroic virtue . . . therein lies the secret of sanctity for all the faithful scattered over the whole world."[5] Pius XI, who canonized her and named her the "star of his pontificate" said that she gives us "an example that everyone in the entire world can and ought to follow."[6] Pius XII, who named her copatroness of France with St. Joan of Arc, stated: "Her way of spiritual childhood, it is the very Gospel, the heart of the Gospels which she has rediscovered."[7] And Pope John XXIII, who, while Papal Nuncio to France, made five pilgrimages to her tomb, said: "I shall never cease exalting the Great Little Saint—the favorable star of my mission in France."

This is unstinted praise and recommendation—and from indisputable authority. But now the uneasy question asserts itself. Have the Popes presented for our imitation a "plaster of Paris saint" (a frequent phrase of the critics), someone whose personality and message have become so disfigured by a group of well-meaning nuns that we have not known until recently what she was really like, what actually made her a saint? Or, worse yet, have the Church authorities in Rome, who, during the process of canonization, had complete access to the unedited manuscript and the actual photographs, who severely interrogated all the witnesses at the Carmel and elsewhere under solemn oath—have they known that a fraud was perpetrated, that a completely distorted image of a saint was propagated, and have they still permitted it without comment, without warning, and with apparent approval?

I think not. I think the cries of fraud and distortion of truth are false and misleading. I feel that the critics have committed some serious historical mistakes and have arrived at some erroneous conclusions, which are as frightening and dangerous as they are untrue. This is the conclusion I have reached after careful and deliberate research into every source I could find. It is a study which took me to archives and libraries in France, which even led me into the cloisters of the Lisieux Carmel, to the cell where St. Thérèse lived, the garden where she wrote parts of her autobiography, the small infirmary where she died. It is a study I undertook with no preconceived notions, with no predecided thesis to prove, with an honest intention to let the facts speak for themselves and point to whatever conclusion they would. (And this I find to be one of the main failings of the critics: most of them seem to have begun their evaluations with some point of bias, a bias which obviously must cloud and disfigure the objectivity of any conclusions they might make.)

This book, then, is a report of a search for truth, a search to reconstruct the life and personality and message of a canonized saint. It has been, for me, a fascinating inquiry, possessing something of the intrigue and adventure of a mystery story; and I can only hope that some of this excitement and sense of adventure might be contagious as we attempt to discover the facts and then, fragment by fragment, put together the true portrait of St. Thérèse.

CHAPTER I

REFLECTIONS ON THE FACTS

The search for St. Thérèse has become complicated by the divergent, and oftentimes contradictory portraits presented by different authors. It is remarkable enough that the rather uneventful twenty-four years which comprised her life have been the subject of so many biographies; but it is even more astonishing that these few years have been interpreted in so many different ways.

In view of these varied interpretations, it would be well to pause to consider the responsibilities facing a hagiographer, a biographer of saints. In particular, the factors involved in writing a biography of St. Thérèse and a consideration of the attitude and approach of several of the saint's biographers would also be most appropriate.

A hagiographer is, first of all, an historian, and as such, he is committed to the search for truth. He must attempt to amass as many facts as possible, and he must lay them down one beside another, orderly, objectively, and honestly. He cannot, of course, report all the facts, those thousands and thousands of biographical details, but he should report all the significant and representative facts which help us to re-create the actual historical situation. There is no room here for editorializing about the facts, no room for omitting any facts which might not happen to agree with the author's theories. The omitted fact could very well afford important insight to the historical situation.

Father Robo affords us an example of this kind of literary editorializing found in some of the new biographies of St. Thérèse. He contends that Thérèse's sister, Pauline, studiously rewrote the manuscript of Thérèse's life before its publication; he claims that she "rubbed out or modified without hesitation any sentence or episode that conflicted with the picture of the angelic child she wished the world to accept" (p. 58). Pauline, then, is the villain of the piece as she laboriously constructs *her* image of Thérèse and delivers it to the world. Much of Father Robo's data to support this theory is quoted from Père François' monumental *Manuscrits Autobiographiques de Sainte Thérèse de L'Enfant Jésus*,[1] which he cites frequently. However, there is an important fact in Père François' study that Robo fails to quote—namely, that one Dom Godfrey Madelaine, the prior of a Premonstratensian abbey in Normandy, was the first editor of Thérèse's manuscript. Dom Godfrey made the initial corrections in the manuscript, divided it into chapters, gave the title to it, and outlined further corrections for Pauline to make.[2] But none of this appears in Robo's study (despite the fact that Père François devotes three pages to this material; and that Robo quotes other sections as close as a page away from this material) and thus the complete historical situation is not related. Assuredly, the exact nature of Dom Godfrey's editorial work must be assessed and analyzed, but it does change our evaluation of the episode when we realize that the primary editorial work on Thérèse's manuscript was done by a literate, conscientious prior of a Premonstratensian abbey, and not by the credulous nuns of Lisieux, as the critics claim. It is the biographer's responsibility to give us these facts.

Another literary problem has plagued the biographies of St. Thérèse: the problem of a highly interpretative and personal presentation of the saint, a portrait formed more by the biographer's likes and dislikes than by the available historical evidence. The biographer, of course, must do more then simply present the facts; he must, in addition, try to evaluate them and coordinate them into a logical whole. But this demands the most scrupulous objectivity, the most meticulous care to reconstruct the actual scene. It is like a gigantic jigsaw puzzle in which all the pieces are laid out on a table and then fitted one way and another, studied, placed against this piece and now against that piece, and finally joined together one by one until the whole picture is assembled. As the biographer attempts this task he must disrobe himself of his previous prejudices, and approach his subject in a spirit of receptivity, with a readiness to discover and learn.

In St. Thérèse's case, so many of her biographers evaluate her against the background of their own prejudices and disenchantments, and, of course, the result is distortion. So many of them begin their appraisal with an almost instinctive dislike for St. Thérèse's country, or her milieu, or her historical epoch, or even Thérèse herself. Frau Goerres, for example, writes:

> For let us be honest with ourselves: Who among us normal Christians of the twentieth century has ever read *The Story of a Soul* for the first time without

being disappointed? Who among us has really liked
the book spontaneously, without the air of an uneasy
conscience which leads us modestly to ascribe our
discontent with this famous work to our own inferi-
ority? (p. 7)

(One might answer Goerres' question as to what *normal* Christian really liked Thérèse's autobiography by
saying that, for one, Pope Pius XI appears to have been
enthusiastic about it. He said, in the homily during the
Mass of Canonization: "No one indeed can read this
book, now propagated throughout the whole world, without loving it thoroughly [*quin adamaret*] and returning
to read it again and again with the greatest profit and
joy of soul.")

Goerres continues:

You, the reader, who have been expectantly looking
for some sign of greatness, read on more and more
wearily from page to page. How sweet all this is, how
well meant, how finely observed, how pleasantly nar-
rated—but how "little," here too. This story confines
the heart instead of expanding it. What a narrow
horizon and what a poverty of content. (p. 8)

But a careful reading of Goerres' study reveals the
root of her bias: she is disenchanted with French Catholicism, and especially the French Catholicism of the late
nineteenth century. Thus she describes St. Thérèse living in a "lower middle-class Catholic ghetto of her time,"
and calls her approach to spirituality "the most dubious
and fleeting kind of piety in the history of the Church"
(p. 13). Goerres says that the pious people of nineteenth-
century France are infected with Puritanism and Jansenism (p. 28), and the ordinary layman is guilty of

superstition in "his crippled religious condition" (p. 29). She speaks of the "deeply-rooted possessiveness of the French nation," and Thérèse herself is described as "entirely French, without a tinge of idealism."

Are we, then, to dismiss Frau Goerres as a Francophobe? Not necessarily, for there is a more simple and more human explanation of her uncompromising attitude toward the French situation. Goerres' thinking is basically an extension of traditional Franco-German tensions into the literary arena. The Germans and French are separated by more distance than the few meters that comprise the width of the Rhine, and they have never been completely sympathetic with each other's political philosophy, economic policies, and even religious concepts. These perennial difficulties were intensified to an even greater degree when Frau Goerres wrote her book on St. Thérèse in the early 1940's. Frau Goerres was in the position of a German authoress discussing a French subject, and writing about her during the years when Germany and France were locked in mortal combat. The possibility of maintaining editorial objectivity in such times is extremely remote and it tends to throw into suspicion her criticisms of the French and their culture. Also of interest in this context is the fact that her book has never been published in France.

Our concern here, however, is not Franco-German difficulties, but the art of biography insofar as it is influenced by the author's personal viewpoint. And the history of biographical writing makes it strikingly clear that it can be so influenced. The geographical position from which an author writes, his national origins, and the historical moment at which he composes can all profoundly affect the literary result. Two American biographical studies of our generation might help to illustrate the point in question. Hudson Strode in his

Jefferson Davis, and Carl Sandburg in his *Abraham
Lincoln* both discuss the American political scene immediately prior to the Civil War. Strode, a Southern
writer, portrays Jefferson Davis desperately trying to
prevent the war between the States while he sees Lincoln inexorably moving the nation toward that fate.
Sandburg, on the other hand, depicts Lincoln as the man
of peace, and contends that the fundamental reason for
Davis' election to the presidency of the Confederacy was
the assurance that he would inaugurate hostilities. Here
we have two scholarly authors, both working with, presumably, the same set of facts, and yet both arriving at
different conclusions. One of the two writers—and, conceivably, both of them—would seem to be writing interpretative history.

An antipathy toward an historical figure or his nation-
ality must necessarily force a biographer into some
strange maneuvering. In the case at hand, Frau Goerres
must begin her study burdened with a dislike of the
French scene and Thérèse's association with it. But she is
immediately confronted with an undeniable fact: despite
the fact that Thérèse was French and was thoroughly
immersed in the milieu of her time, she did become a
canonized saint, officially approved by the Church for our
veneration and imitation. Hence the enigma! There is only
one path leading out of Goerres' dilemma and she gladly
takes it—Thérèse's greatness and importance must lie in a
"breakthrough," a radical departure from French thinking. And this is precisely one of Goerres' major theories:
Thérèse became a saint by disassociating herself from the
religious concepts of her family, her epoch, her religious
order, and her nation. Thus, Goerres titles a principal
section of her book "The Breakthrough," and this theme
is continued to the concluding sentences of her study
where she states:

As the perfected butterfly breaks out of the chrysalis, so she emerges transformed from the shrivelling shell of her period and appears before us as the pure embodiment of Christian reality. (p. 413)

And:

She who knew only obedience, only listening, unquestionably accepted the highly questionable elements in her contemporaries' piety. But the burning purity of her touch melted away all the old slag. (p. 414)

Goerres' preoccupation, therefore, is to show us Thérèse emerging from "the shrivelling shell of her period" and melting away "all the old slag." This is a forced thesis, inspired by the author's feeling toward the French, and it is an unhappy example of the interpretative biography to which St. Thérèse has been subjected.

The saint, however, is more than a simple historical figure, and this is what makes his biography so challenging and difficult. In evaluating a saint, we are attempting to understand a person who lived on two planes: the natural *and* the supernatural. We are dealing with a two-dimensional figure, a true human being equipped with human nature and involved in human situations, but one who lives concomitantly in the world of grace.

According to Catholic theology, habitual grace is a created gift of God which inheres in the soul and makes man, to some degree, a participator in the Divine Nature. The person possessing grace, therefore, has been raised to a new plane of existence on which he lives and operates. There is, within him, a new source of life—in fact, a new *kind* of life—and it has been popularly explained by saying that there is as much difference between a man who possesses grace and one who does not as there is between a man and an animal.

The saint lives this life of grace completely, to an eminent and heroic degree, allowing it to become the source of strength for his spiritual activities and the final motivation for them. Thus, the saint's biographer is confronted with the added difficulty of studying two lives—the human life and the life of grace—in order to arrive at a full understanding of the complete person. The problem is compounded by the fact that, in the saint, there is no cleavage, no dichotomy, between these two lives. The saint does not operate sometimes under the force of his human nature, and at other times under the impulse of grace; rather, these two lives are fused into one so that, while remaining a complete human being, the saint is continually operating under the influence of divine grace. In observing a saint, then, we are witnessing God's activity in the human soul. And this is what intrigues us and inspires us—we watch someone like us struggling through our poor human clay until he emerges to touch the stars, to see God, to live with Him. We are observing, as the old peasant said of the Curé of Ars, God in a man.

This aspect of the saint's life is what so completely fascinated the early hagiographers, and what caused so many poor and unrealistic biographies. Biographers became so impressed by the divine element in the saint's life that they omitted the human element and unwittingly became proponents of a division, or even a hostility, between the life of nature and the life of grace. The early hagiographers were concerned only with the miraculous, the heroic, and sometimes the bizarre. They obscured the true notion of sanctity—fidelity to grace, observance of the commandments, and friendship with God—and left the unfortunate impression that the saint was some superhuman miracle worker endowed with heroic power and an astonishing strength of will. For this reason, biographies of the saints became clogged with accounts of miracles, many of them pure legends, and the narratives seemed to be one account of strenuous and superhuman activity after another. The hagiographer's purpose was in discovering, and sometimes inventing, the divine in the saint's life. Certainly, the intention was noble, insofar as it reminded readers of this necessary dimension in their lives, the divine. But it was bad biography—because the saints were also human.

Modern hagiography has sought to remedy this situation, to present a more realistic and accurate picture of the saints. In this endeavor, the modern biographer has been assisted by more critical and more valid procedures of historical research, but his greatest help has come from a clearer understanding of biography's objectives. The modern author is concerned—and rightly so—with presenting the saint as a true human being in whom grace operates, unimpeded and unobstructed. In investigating a saint, both the human element *and* the divine element are discovered, and then studied to show how they are joined in the one person to produce the true historical figure.

There has been, however, one unfortunate tendency in modern hagiography, something that perhaps was almost inevitable. Some modern writers, in their honest attempts to correct the mistakes of the earlier biographies, have allowed the pendulum to swing to the opposite extreme. Dissatisfied with studies that showed the saints as supermen, they have tried to portray the saints as thoroughly human, with human instincts and human ambitions and human faults. This is a laudable and necessary objective, and we have benefited immensely from these studies which give us more biographical data about the saints. But many of these studies have concerned themselves *only* with the human element in the saints' lives, relegating the divine element to a negligible position. It is a reaction against earlier hagiography, and as so often happens in human affairs, reactions can be violent things, terminating in equally erroneous positions on the opposite extreme.

A failure to consider the operation of grace in a saint can only lead to a distorted picture. First, because there is an omission of historical data. Grace, in the saint's life, is factual, something that actually occurred; and it cannot be considered a minor historical fact, since it shapes and forms the saint to such an important degree. Any attempt to evaluate the saint without including the action of God's grace is bound to produce a truncated and incomplete portrait. Secondly, and more seriously, gross misinterpretations will result from this method because the effects of grace in the life and personality of the saint will then be considered mere natural phenomena and judged according to simple human norms. It is impossible to evaluate grace adequately through psychology, history, or any other human science. Unless a theological viewpoint is employed, many aspects of the saint's life will be misunderstood, or even considered abnormal and unhealthy. This is what occurred in that long historical dispute about St. Teresa of Avila when a number of non-Catholic scholars, employing only history and psychology, judged her to be an hysteric beset with hallucinations.

Some of St. Thérèse's biographers have failed her in this regard. They have preoccupied themselves so much with the good and necessary tools of historical research that they have omitted that second dimension in her life, divine grace. Ida Goerres, for example, says:

Now hagiography has become biography of a canonized individual; history and psychology hold the floor, and the attempt is made to set forth and explain the sanctity of a saint as if it were the accomplishment of any other famous person: from heredity, environment, education, encounters, crises, aids, hinderances and inevitable catastrophes, and from sociological and historical conditions. (p. 397)

Goerres' statement is deceptive: it is good as far as it goes, but it does not go far enough. The areas of research she mentions are invaluable and should all be used, but more than this is necessary if we are to understand St. Thérèse, or any of the saints. Goerres says, "the attempt is made to set forth and explain the sanctity of a saint as if it were the accomplishment of any other famous person." And that is precisely the problem, because sanctity is not like the accomplishment of any other famous person; sanctity is the full flowering of God's grace in the soul and the heroic practice of the virtues, and a special viewpoint is necessary to understand and appreciate this.

Hans von Balthasar, a German theologian writing after World War II, has criticized this whole method. "This psychological approach has been so much overdone that it needs complementing and correcting by the principles of theology," he states.[3] Balthasar recognizes the benefits that new biographical procedures have given to hagiography, but he insists that the most valuable tool will always be theology. He quotes Philipon's statement: "Everyone naturally demands that a nerve-specialist who is telling us about one of his patients should know his psychiatry, but no one seems to assume that a person has to be a theologian before speaking of God's workings in the souls of saints."[4]

And these workings of God in the saints' souls are what

most interest us in studying their lives. Otherwise, why would we even bother to consider a girl like Thérèse, a sweet, smiling, quiet-living child from the provinces? Apart from her spiritual development, what could we possibly find of interest in her story? If we prescind from divine grace, Abraham Lincoln would be a much more majestic and attractive personality than she; and Anne Frank, who died in the concentration camp at Belsen, would be a more tragic and appealing figure. Assuredly, we want to know all we can about her—what she did, what she looked like, how she reacted to situations—but our principal concern is how this real and historical person cooperated with God's grace in becoming a saint.

If the biographer prescinds from the workings of grace in St. Thérèse's soul, he finds himself with a literary problem: there is not much else of interest or importance in the life of this middle-class Norman girl. It is then that literary invention takes over: drama and conflict must be painted into her ordinary and prosaic little life, or Thérèse herself must be made to appear a figure of personal tragedy, struggling against her melancholia and mental difficulties. This is the only path open if one would write an interesting biography, and it is the path so many biographers have trod. Thus, Balthasar claims that Goerres studies Thérèse in the light of German personalism, and "in accordance with the ideals of the *Jugendbewegung* Ida Goerres takes as her negative thesis the breakaway from ecclesiastical and ascetical formalism and the rediscovery of personal integrity."[5] In summarizing his evaluation of Goerres' study, he states:

. . . she has to resort to depth psychology in order to bring out her heroine's greatness. This leads to obvious misinterpretations, so that in spite of her brilliant account of Thérèse's personal life and milieu Goerres' work is inadequate on the theological side.[6]

These new biographers are looking for a perspective, a place to stand in viewing Thérèse's life. They have chosen a host of perspectives—psychology, history, and sociology among them—but they have either omitted theology or relegated it to a minor position. Distortion has been the result, for a limited viewpoint can only produce a limited portrait.

The hagiographer, in evaluating the life of a canonized saint, has at his disposal a tool of immense value not possessed by the ordinary biographer: he is studying someone whose life and activities have been thoroughly investigated by the Church with the most scrupulous care. The results of this research are available to the hagiographer, and in the case of the modern saints it is an amazing research. Since the legislation of Pope Urban VIII in the seventeenth century and Pope Benedict XIV in the eighteenth century, the life of the candidate for canonization is subjected to the most painstaking inquiry: evidence is amassed, witnesses are interrogated, writings are studied. In fact, an actual trial is conducted according to regular juridical procedures. The value of this ecclesiastical trial is enhanced by the fact that the witnesses testify under oath and they all receive a precept, binding under penalty of excommunication, to tell the truth and to discuss their testimony with no one else. The record of this trial and the juridical decision about it is published in two large volumes called the *Processus* which is printed in a carefully limited edition and usually distributed only to those who have some close connection with the case. There are, for example, only about seventy-five copies of St. Thérèse's *Processus* extant in the world today.

Thus the hagiographer often finds himself in a privi-

leged condition compared with the regular biographer.
How much more complete a biography could be written
about, say, Alexander Hamilton if we had the record of
a posthumous trial about his life in which his contemporaries related their recollections of him under oath.
(Needless to state, no biography of a modern saint could
be considered satisfactory or complete unless the
Processus were employed.)

The *Processus* of one saint is sometimes more valuable
than that of another, depending on how soon after the
candidate's death the investigation is begun. Frequently,
no contemporaries of the saint are still living at the time
of the trial. The preliminary investigations about St.
Thérèse were begun within ten years after her death and
the great majority of people who knew her intimately
were able to testify at her trial. This is extremely help-
ful to the biographers of St. Thérèse, especially since the
witnesses at her trial were devout and religious people—
in fact, most of them were cloistered nuns—and it can be
reasonably presumed that the threat of excommunication prodded the majority of them, at least, into telling
what they thought to be the truth.

Furthermore, the *Processus* affords one other invaluable
advantage: the witnesses are asked to testify not only
about their recollection of specific incidents in the life of
the candidate, but also about their *general conclusions*
of the individual's character and personality. The importance of this can be ascertained when we consider
that one of the biographer's pitfalls is the anecdote-to-
general-conclusion process by which an anecdote or two
is cited and a general conclusion immediately drawn.
Bad biography is replete with this process: an incident or
anecdote is related and then the biographer quickly states
that we have gained an understanding of character and
personality of the individual under study. It could very

well be true that the single incident does illustrate a general pattern of behavior, but it could be equally true that the incident must be studied against the total picture of the person's life since it could have been a solitary episode or something wrenched out of context or misunderstood by the biographer. The *Processus,* however, allows the witnesses to recall their specific remembrances, but it also allows them to state their general evaluations, too. And biography is the beneficiary. We might, for example, find an episode in the life of St. X in which he appears to be acting rather gruffly and highhandedly in some situation, but on the other hand we had some thirty-five witnesses, all close associates of St. X, who state that he was an extremely kind person in dealing with people. We have no hesitancy in concluding, then, that whatever be the meaning of the single incident, St. X was habitually a kind person. This is the kind of service the *Processus* renders.

The Church is not historically naïve in accepting the evidence and testimony which has been amassed; rather, to avoid being credulous, the ecclesiastical authorities are severely critical of all the evidence and only accept it when it has been proved beyond any reasonable doubt. This position of critical doubt and suspension of assent is adopted in a special manner by the Promoter of the Faith, popularly known as the Devil's Advocate. The Devil's Advocate—in St. Thérèse's cause, Msgr. Angelo Mariani —is the ecclesiastical judge appointed by the Congregation of Rites to argue against the canonization and to propose every rational objection to it. He sifts and combs the testimony, studies the writings, and prepares a careful brief stating the reasons against the canonization. The Congregation must then appoint a committee to answer the objections in writing. The brief of the Devil's Advocate and the response to it are both studied by the judges of the Congregation and the Pope himself, and only when every objection has been completely and satisfactorily answered can the cause proceed.

The work of the Devil's Advocate is no feeble gesture, no mere pose, but rather it is a rigorous historical scrutiny geared to unearthing every bit of evidence, no matter how unpleasant or unsavory it may be. The reason for the establishment of a Devil's Advocate is twofold: first, it guarantees a forum in which any controversial evidence must be introduced and must be answered before the cause can proceed; secondly, it attempts to foresee all conceivable objections to the cause which could possibly be made at some later date and to answer them *before* the canonization. It is this latter aspect that is especially interesting in the case of St. Thérèse, since the great majority of the new revelations or new insights being presented about St. Thérèse today were first considered thirty-five or forty years ago by the Devil's Advocate.

The thoroughness with which the Devil's Advocate did his work in the cause of St. Thérèse is astonishing; he omitted not the slightest shred of evidence which could be used against the canonization. Some of the charges concern minute, infinitesimal points, and they are almost ludicrous, but they do demonstrate the thoroughness of his accomplishment. For example, in one of her letters St. Thérèse wrote about her father: "Is there anyone on earth whom God loves more than my dear Father? I cannot believe so." The Devil's Advocate pounced on this phrase, accusing her of exaggeration and theological error since, as he stated, no one can know in this life whom God actually loves the most. The response by Msgr. Toeschi of the Congregation of Rites is a calm and human answer, claiming that Thérèse's words are not to be taken in the strict literal sense since a child can speak of her father with love and some excess; and, he adds, perhaps she did understand her father's outstanding virtue better than anyone else.

There are many other small points like the above which were raised by the Devil's Advocate, but some of his objections concerned more important and more serious issues—namely that Thérèse did not enjoy a good reputation in the convent, that she did not possess the virtue of humility, that she refused spiritual direction, that she was insubordinate to the superior of her convent, that her cause for canonization was contrived and arranged by the propagandizing efforts of the Lisieux Carmel. For anyone familiar with the recent literature on St. Thérèse, these are not unfamiliar charges; they are being presented today as fresh discoveries, new revelations which give us a better understanding of the real Thérèse. And as we view the marked similarity between the charges of the Devil's Advocate and the recent studies on St. Thérèse we are, first of all, gratified by the efficiency of the Devil's Advocate who anticipated all these charges and presented the opportunity of having them discussed and answered before the canonization. But, then, we might be somewhat dismayed that recent writers have felt compelled to resurrect these old charges and assume the role of latter-day Devil's Advocates, expecially since all those objections have been handled to the satisfaction of the Holy See.

The Church, however, offers a more important service to the biographer than the simple presentation of historical data: it brings its infallible authority to bear in the final decision about the sanctity of an individual. This is, of course, a service which is of value to those who have faith and who comprehend the Church's role in the world; but then, it is for the faithful, principally, that the saints are canonized.

Papal infallibility is, of course, no all-embracing prerogative of the Pope applicable to every phase of his life, but rather is something employed by him in certain prescribed areas concerning faith and morals, *The canonization of a saint is one of those areas.*[7] In the Bull of Canonization for St. Thérèse, Pope Pius XI asserts in strong language the tenor of his pronouncement:

> No one is permitted to contradict or disagree with this letter of Our definition, Our decree, Our mandate, and Our wish; but if anyone temerariously dares to attempt that, let him know that he has incurred the wrath of the Omnipotent God and His Holy Apostles, Peter and Paul.[8]

For the professional theologian, this is the language of an infallible decree, despite the fact that the precise term is not used. In other decrees of canonization Pius XI does use the explicit terms of infallibility; for example, in the canonization of St. Maria Micaela of the Blessed Sacrament, the nineteenth-century Spanish saint, he states:

> . . . We, from the chair of Blessed Peter, as the supreme head of the universal Catholic Church, pronounce this infallible statement in these words . . .[9]

The reason for an infallible pronouncement in this matter is readily apparent. Having admitted the fact of papal infallibility, it becomes necessary to extend it to the canonization of a saint since this is something that intimately pertains to faith and morals. The Church presents the saints to us for our imitation and veneration, and she proposes them to us as models of Christian virtue upon whom we can pattern our lives without any doubt or hesitation. But if the Church were to err in this regard, if she were to propose unworthy and misleading models to us, she would be unfaithful to her mission, she would be leading us astray in the vital matter of eternal salvation. For this reason—as the doctrine of theologians and the Papal documents themselves teach us—the Church presents its saints to the world relying on the full inspiration and the unerring support of the Holy Spirit.

The Catholic hagiographer, therefore, has some irrefutable facts at hand as he begins his study. He knows that the subject of his investigation is certainly in heaven, and he knows that his subject has, as the documents of canonization testify, practiced heroic virtue in his life. Ordinarily, this does not provide any particular illumination for the Catholic hagiographer since he is readily willing to accept these facts and use them to guide his study. But occasionally the new hagiography seems to call some of these facts into question, particularly those concerning the heroism of the saint's virtues.

The precise meaning of the term "heroic virtue" has been the object of much theological discussion and some dispute. Whatever the full implications of the term may be, it certainly means that the saint possessed true virtue —especially the theological virtues of faith, hope, and charity, and the moral virtues of prudence, justice, fortitude, and temperance—and practiced them to an eminent degree. If a biographer were to deny, therefore, the existence of some theological or moral virtue in a particular canonized saint, he would be placing himself in direct opposition to the Church's decree of canonization and he would find himself in the uncomfortable position of denying the Church's infallible authority. If, for example, someone were to argue that St. Thérèse did not possess the true virtue of humility, his assertion would be inadmissible from the Church's viewpoint since the Act of Canonization specifically states that she did possess the virtue of humility, as well as the other moral and theological virtues.

Another aspect of the Church's act of canonization presents itself, something which does not lend itself to such sharp distinctions as the above: namely, the image of the saint presented by the Church in its official canonization process. And here we touch a vital point in St. Thérèse's case, since so many of our recent biographies of her contend that her image has been a false or misleading one. This contention is rooted in the erroneous assumption that our picture of St. Thérèse was proposed to the faithful by the nuns at Lisieux, and then seconded or approved by the Holy See; in actuality, it was the Holy See which proposed Thérèse to the world, despite whatever propagandizing efforts had been previously undertaken by the Lisieux Carmel. No group or organization in the Church has the power or authority to propose a saint to the universal Church. A group might perhaps publish biographies and studies of an individual, try to incite interest, and even request an investigation by the Holy See, but in the final analysis the Holy See must, through its delegates, conduct its own investigation, make its own decisions, and publish its own conclusions about the life and spirit of the saint. These conclusions are contained in the *Super Dubio* decree about the heroism of the saint's virtues, the decrees for the beatification and canonization, and in the Pope's homily at the Mass of canonization, all of which are published in that official medium of promulgation, the *Acta Apostolicae Sedis*. In St. Thérèse's case, these documents contain a résumé of her life, an interpretation of some of the more significant events, and an analysis of her spirit and importance. These decrees, parts of which we will cite later on, should be extremely valuable to the Catholic biographer: first, because they represent years of exhaustive research and study; and secondly, because they assuredly must be guided to some degree by the Holy Spirit Who abides in the Church and directs it in selecting and proposing its saints.

We have already indicated the extent of the Church's historical research into the life of a saint, a research which is far more detailed and complete than could possibly be done by any biographer. From this viewpoint alone, the decrees in the *Acta* should command the hagiographer's respect and attention. But—the more thorny problem—what degree of religious belief, if any, does the Catholic owe these documents? Surely, the historical part of the Pope's decree of canonization is not an infallible statement fortified by the papal prerogative of infallibility, but does that mean we are free to dismiss it? Does it mean we may regard it as an historically naïve and credulous document? Does it mean, in St. Thérèse's case, that the Pope could have presented to the Church an inaccurate and false image, an image which bore little resemblance to the real historical person? It would hardly seem so. It would seem, on the contrary, that the Holy Spirit must guide the Holy See in its investigations so that the image proposed to the faithful for their imitation should correspond, at least in its principal outlines, to the true person.

This is a question which requires much more study by professional theologians, and since the *Humani Generis* of Pius XII the whole question of the assent due to papal documents is being re-examined. But until we can obtain more precise answers, might we suggest that some type of what the theologians call "religious assent" is due to the image of a saint presented by the Church? This would seem to follow from the seriousness of the matter and from the fact that these decrees are published in the *Acta*

Apostolicae Sedis (and the professional theologian is aware of the reverence owed to papal documents published in the *Acta*). At any rate, it would appear rash and imprudent for any hagiographer to place himself in the position of contradicting these official decrees and asserting that the Church has presented a false image of the saint.

St. Thérèse has been called a "hagiographical wonder," since few saints in the entire history of the Church have been the subject of so many biographies and studies. Her unique appeal to the modern world is undoubtedly responsible for much of that, but no small part of the literary curiosity she has aroused must be ascribed to the fact that we possess an amazing amount of information and data about her, perhaps more than about any other saint. A large percentage of the people who knew her were able to testify at her trial; the majority of her letters are extant; and we have her autobiography, that astonishingly frank and candid piece of writing. However, it is this very mass of historical documentation which has been responsible for so many conflicting theories about her. Where we have had less information about some saints, there was less room for inventiveness, less opportunity for the biographer to select facts conformable to his personal theories. This does not mean we should regret the documentation at our disposal, it only means we should be more keenly aware of the biographer's task and his responsibilities.

These are basic considerations binding on anyone attempting to tell St. Thérèse's story. When any of these facts are overlooked or slighted, then inevitably the portrait presented is inadequate and, indeed, in some cases distorted. Obviously, these are matters which must be kept to the fore in our quest for the true St. Thérèse.

CHAPTER II

THE CHILD

1. FRENCH FAMILY MARTIN

On the thirteenth of July, 1858, Louis Martin and Zélie Guérin were married in the Church of Notre Dame at Alençon. Their union, which endured nineteen years until Mme. Martin's death in 1877, was a prolific one, but it was also an important one from the viewpoint of ecclesiastical history, since it produced a canonized saint. The origins of a saint are always of considerable interest and pertinence in reconstructing the portrait of a saint, and this is particularly true in St. Thérèse's case because she was so intimately immersed in the life of her family, so deeply attached to it, and so profoundly affected by it. Thérèse herself stated that she found it difficult to understand those saints who appeared as if they possessed little love for their families; and her love for her own family—for her parents and her four sisters—intensified and deepened over the years.

Whatever else Thérèse Martin became in life, she never for one moment ceased to be a girl from the provinces, a child of Normandy. She was born there, died there, and except for a four-week trip to Rome, spent her entire life there. Normandy was then, as it is today, an eternal place, constantly reverting to the gentle rhythm of its calm life, despite the soldiers who have marched through it and the bombs which have fallen on it. It is an imperturbable place of rolling hills and hedgerows and rich farmland and multicolored flowers and quiet towns.

The province of the 1870's was recovering from German occupation, the result of Bismarck's crushing defeat of the French armies in the Franco-Prussian War. By the terms of the Treaty of Frankfurt, France was obliged to pay a war indemnity of five billion francs, and the German troops remained in occupation until the sum was finally paid in 1873, the very year of Thérèse's birth. Thus, Thérèse was born in an era of reconstruction, at the inaugural of the Third Republic; she would witness the first shaky years of that Republic, she would see the intense struggle between Royalists and Republicans, and she would view with apprehension the mounting anti-Catholicism in France. She would live only twenty-four years, spending them all in two small towns in northwestern France, but during those twenty-four years she became a saint.

There are marked similarities in the backgrounds of her parents, Louis and Zélie Martin: they were both children of professional soldiers who fought in Napoleon's army, they both considered a religious vocation in their earlier lives, they were both successful in the commercial world before their marriage, and they were both extremely pious. Zélie Guérin was born on December 23, 1831, in the Norman village of Gandelain, and when her father retired to Alençon she attended school there at the Convent of Perpetual Adoration. Some time in her late teens she applied for admission to the Sisters of Charity, but the Mother Superior declined to accept her for a reason of which we have no record. It was a bitter disappointment for the young girl, and all her life she nurtured the secret hope that when her children had been raised she might be able to spend the final years of her life in a convent. She took lessons in lacemaking and began to produce at home the delicate *point d'Alençon,* the fine lace for which the town is noted. Her enterprise was successful and by the time of her marriage she had a thriving business, employing a group of women who worked in their individual homes and produced lace which she assembled and sold to Paris and the larger cities.

Louis Martin was born at Bordeaux on August 22, 1823, and he also reached Alençon when his father retired from the army. At nineteen Louis spent some months at his cousin's house in Rennes, Brittany; the cousin, Louis Bohard, was a watchmaker, and from him Louis learned the rudiments of the trade he was to practice for thirty years. A few years later he took an extended trip through Switzerland, arrived at the Augustinian monastery of St. Bernard in the Pennine Alps, became fascinated by the monk's life, and decided to seek admission. However, he was refused, at least until he could master Latin, a language in which he had received little training. Upon his return to Alençon, he engaged a tutor and embarked on a vigorous program of study, but after a year and a half he discontinued it and apparently relinquished any further ideas of a religious vocation. Father Piat, in his *The Story of a Family,* states that poor health made Louis give up his studies,[1] while Ida Goerres, who seems to have a particular disaffection for Louis Martin, says, ". . . he had not the character which enables many whose vocation comes to them late in life to resume and carry through the struggle with school books" (p. 31). Neither statement can be proved, nor it is important to do so, but we might note that Louis was only twenty-two when he made application to the Augustinians. We could ask if it is necessary to give precise and weighty reasons for Louis' discontinuance of studies; might we not simply say that he decided not to become a priest?

Louis spent the next three years in Paris, studying his craft, and when he returned to Alençon he was a master watchmaker and jeweler. His business prospered, and he seemed quite content to remain a bachelor. Zélie Guérin's house was on the opposite side of town, and only a chance meeting in 1858 on one of the town bridges introduced the jeweler and the lacemaker. One of the stories about Zélie Guérin—again, a story which is impossible to prove or disprove—contends that she heard an interior voice that day on the bridge urging her to marry Louis Martin. A rapid courtship followed, and three months later they were married. Louis was thirty-four, and Zélie was twenty-six.

Louis and Zélie Martin present a study in distinct and, in many ways, contradictory personalities. Louis was a tall, quiet man, with soft brown eyes and a chestnut-colored beard which framed his face. He was gentle, amiable, and somewhat shy; he liked fishing, solitary walks in the country, and all his life he remained an enthusiastic traveler. Zélie, on the other hand, was a vigorous, forthright, active person, much more agressive than her husband, despite the fact that she traveled little and preferred to remain in the busy circle of her home. She was small of stature, with an alert, attractive face, sharp black eyes, hair worn in a knot at the nape of her neck. The distinct temperaments of the Martins were brought into sharp relief by the testimony given at St. Thérèse's trial for canonization. The four surviving daughters all testified to their parents' extraordinary piety and to the close bond of affection in the family, but they were careful to note the differences between Louis and Zélie Martin. Céline, for example, says of her father: "When I want to imagine St. Joseph, I think of my father. His heart had an exceptional tenderness towards us, and he lived for us." But, summarizing Zélie's temperament, she states: "My mother had a superior intelligence and extraordinary energy. Nothing was too difficult for her." The phrase "extraordinary energy" recurs frequently in the testimony. Pauline, years later when she had become Mother Agnes, Superior of the Carmel of Lisieux, said: "My mother was abnegation personified; she had an extraordinary energy." One begins to feel that the phrase characterized Zélie Martin for her four daughters.

Zélie continued her lace business after her marriage, moving her equipment into the front room of Louis' house on the Rue du Pont Neuff in Alençon. That she was able to manage a business, run a home, and raise a family is just one more proof of her "extraordinary energy." In 1870, twelve years after his marriage, Louis sold his watchmaker's shop to his nephew, and devoted his full time to managing Zélie's lace business. Thus he was only forty-seven when he retired from his own enterprise, but it had been a rewarding one for him. Céline said that he had gained a fortune "which, without being immense, gave her parents a very honorable position." Abbé Dumaine, the parish priest of Alençon, said that M. Martin had obtained "a rather sizeable fortune." His decision to join Zélie in her work was prompted by their individual preferences in the business world: Zélie preferred the productive aspect, while Louis liked merchandising and sales. Zélie confined herself, then, to producing and assembling the lace, and Louis sold it, contacting merchants, conducting the correspondence, and journeying to Paris. This mutually satisfactory arrangement continued until Zélie's death seven years later, at which time M. Martin retired from the business world completely.

Zélie's character is more easy to sketch since it is less complicated than that of her husband. We can follow her in an almost direct line through the years of her marriage: the devoted mother and wife, the tireless worker, the sick woman plagued with cancer of the breast, fulfilling her obligations resolutely, pale, fatigued, resigned to her early death at forty-five. Louis is a multifaceted character, more liable to misinterpretation since he can be viewed from a number of different angles. Ida Goerres sees him as a "taciturn and dreamy solitary" (p. 33) and "a dreamer and brooder, an idealist and romantic" (p. 34). This is more caricature than portrait and represents an unfortunate tendency to present Louis Martin as a weak and evanescent character. In actuality, despite his quiet disposition, he was a strong and virile person. He was a volunteer fireman who once dragged an old woman out of a burning building, he was credited with saving several people from drowning, and during the Franco-Prussian War when he was too old for the army he volunteered and served as a military scout in the woods near Alençon. During the occupation of Alençon a German soldier attempted to steal some jewelry from his store and M. Martin fought him off, ejected him from the premises, and lodged a complaint with the German commandant against the plundering soldier. He was fifty years old when Thérèse was born, and shortly afterwards he retired from business; thus in those later years we find him in a less vigorous and more tranquil period of his life. He devoted more time to fishing, and was able to indulge further his passion for travel, journeying to Rome, Germany, Austria, Constantinople, and the pilgrimage sites of Lourdes and Chartres. Those last years of his life also gave him the opportunity for a deeper spiritual life through prayer, reading, and solitude. He enjoyed an excellent reputation, and Pére Pichon, the Jesuit, called him "a venerable patriarch." Abbé Dumaine recalls: "He loved to employ his leisure time at fishing, often in the company of the parish priest, and he usually gave whatever he caught to the Poor Clare sisters in Alençon. He was esteemed by everybody; he was a perfect, honest man." Marceline Husé, a chambermaid at the Guérin's house in Lisieux, said of him: "M. Martin was esteemed in Lisieux as a patriarch of old, and as a saint." And Céline sums up her recollections of her father:

My father had an admirable charity for his neighbor, and he never said the least unkind thing about anyone. He excused everybody's faults and never permitted us to criticize anybody. He had a profound veneration for all priests. It was said of him that he was a saint.

Louis and Zélie Martin enjoyed that rich and sometimes rare blessing, a happy family life. Despite their divergent temperaments and the casualness of their meeting, they found themselves eminently suited for each other and very deeply in love. Speaking of the Martins, Abbé Dumaine said: "The union in that family was remarkable—between the husband and wife, and between the parents and their children." Perhaps the most striking articulation of the love that inhabited the Martin household is contained in some of the extant correspondence between Zélie and Louis. In 1873, Mme. Martin took Pauline and Marie with her for a short visit to her brother's home in Lisieux, and she wrote to her husband:

My dear Louis,

We arrived yesterday afternoon at half past four; my brother met us at the station and was delighted to see us. Both he and his wife are doing everything to entertain us. . . . The children are in raptures, and their happiness will be complete if the weather is fine. . . . I feel just like the fish you take out of water; they are no longer in their element and must perish.

This would have the same effect on me if my stay had to be very prolonged. I feel ill at ease. I am not in my niche, and that overflows into the physical sphere and I feel almost ill. However, I reason with myself and try to master the feeling. I am with you all day in spirit, and say to myself: "Now he is doing such and such a thing."

I long to be with you, Louis dear. I love you with all my heart and I feel my affection doubled by being deprived of your company. I could not live apart from you. . . .

I embrace you as I love you. The little girls wish me to tell you that they are enjoying themselves at Lisieux and send you a big hug.[2]

And in the same vein, M. Martin wrote home to his wife when he was away on a business trip in 1863:

Dearest,

I cannot arrive at Alençon before Monday. The time passes slowly, for I long to be with you.

I need not say I was very pleased to receive your letter, except that I see by it that you are overtiring yourself. So I recommend calm and moderation, above all in your lace work. I have some orders for the *Compagnie Lyonnaise*. Once more, do not worry so much.

With God's help, we shall manage to keep up a nice little home. . . .

I kiss you all lovingly, whilst awaiting the pleasure of being with you again. I hope Marie and Pauline are being very good!

Your husband and true friend who loves you forever.[3]

The love between Zélie and Louis naturally influenced the whole tenor of the home and the relationship between parents and children. Léonie, the middle daughter, said: "Our parents loved their children tenderly." This undoubtedly had a profound influence in shaping the future St. Thérèse, who wrote in her autobiography:

All my life God surrounded me with love, and my earliest recollections are those of smiles and the most tender caresses.

Louis and Zélie were, furthermore, deeply religious. The witnesses at the trial—the four daughters, Abbé Dumaine, Père Pichon, Marceline Husé, and Dom Godfrey Madelaine—all arrive at the same conclusion: the parents were extremely pious themselves and gave their children a solid education in Christian principles. There are stories of the couple attending six o'clock Mass each morning and receiving Communion as frequently as possible; the constant, hidden acts of charity they performed; the solicitude for the poor; their diligence at fasting during Lent (this seems to have made a strong impression on the four daughters, because they all mention it); the faithful observance of the Sabbath; the family prayers. In fact, Pope Pius XI, in the Apostolic Brief for St. Thérèse's beatification, called the Martin household: *A home of piety.*[4]

The Martins were economically in what we would today call, at the very least, the upper middle class. They were of the *bourgeoisie*, thoroughly French, and thoroughly Victorian. They had full-time maids, never permitted the girls to go anywhere unchaperoned, taught them all to dabble in painting, a little music, and fine needlework. Their recreations consisted of song fests at home in the evenings, picnics in the country, an occasional trip to a pilgrimage site, and an annual trip to the beaches where, all swathed in Victorian beach gear, they sat demurely on the sand. The photographs we have of the Martins and their neighbors show us the girls in their subdued dresses, tightly corseted, their hair usually combed straight back into a bun. This was the plush and mahogany age, the prim and starched Victorian era so far removed from our modern thinking. Thérèse was completely immersed in that era and thoroughly indoctrinated by it. She evidences it by her vocabulary, her manner of expression, and her almost coy viewpoint. And it is this which hinders so many people from appreciating Thérèse; it is all too cozy, too pretty, too stuffy, like something out of a Louisa May Alcott book.

It has become almost mandatory, it would seem, to begin any consideration of St. Thérèse with a strong denunciation of the Victorian society and a protestation that Thérèse should be considered apart from her background. That is probably legitimate, since Thérèse is a saint for the ages and was not canonized for her Victorian background, and certainly no one is compelled to like that era. But, as we read these strong denunciations, one begins to wonder how much of them represents original thinking and how much represents mere parrot-like repetition of previous thinking. At the risk of appearing chauvinistic and unmodern, might we suggest that there are commendable aspects of the *fin de siècle* society; that, despite the plush and mahogany, those people possessed some values we have lost; that, while there is much to laugh at, there is much to admire. We smile at the tightly corseted women with their unbelievable hats, and we talk of progress and emancipation. But, as we scan the years that separate us from that era, do we really find so much true progress in the position of womanhood? Was the jazz-age woman, with her bobbed hair and jangling beads and short skirts, so much more attractive than the tranquil—and, granted, rather stuffy—lady of the Victorian age? Or was the lady riveter during the Second World War? Or is the suburban housewife, with her frenetic activity and her sleeping pills? Are modern women any more happy or adjusted? Or could it possibly be that the *fin de siècle* women, despite all their comical aspects, attained a greater degree of happiness with their close family circles and their homey virtues? These are questions to ponder. And they do not admit of glib answers.

In Alençon, and later in Lisieux, the Martins lived a close, circumscribed life, even more so than that of their neighbors. They were a unit sufficient unto themselves. We have seen how Zélie's whole life was absorbed in her home and her children, and this left her little time, or inclination, for outside interests. Louis, however, did have broader contacts. He liked to travel, as we have observed; he sought companions for his fishing; he was one of the founders of the Catholic Club in Alençon. But, in the main, his chief interests were in the home, too. The Martins did little visiting, and, apart from the parish priests, few people were invited to their home. Was this poor pedagogy on the parents' part? Some commentators have thought so, especially in light of Thérèse's poor adjustment at school later on. It is difficult to judge with any certainty, although it does seem that the arrangement was happy and satisfactory. One point should be noted, though: it was by preference, rather than command, that the family was so close-knit. As one reads through the testimony at the trial one receives the impression that there was no program to shelter the children, nor was there any proscription of outside activities; it was simply that they all preferred each other's company. Abbé Dumaine, speaking of the five sisters, commented: "The children were fine students and they remained to themselves mostly; they all had the same tastes and the same Christian habits, and they liked to remain together." We get glimpses of the Martins at home in the evening: they sang songs together; they played draughts; M. Martin did imitations with his talent for mimicry, a talent which Thérèse inherited and later used to amuse the nuns in the convent; they read aloud each evening from Gueranger's *Liturgical Year,* and sometimes from a novel borrowed at the parish library. By our standards it sounds singularly unexciting, but nevertheless it was part of the fabric of a happy home.

The Martins have been accused of bad pedagogy in a more serious matter: the question of being Puritanical and Jansenistic. We might say, first of all, that this accusation is an occupational hazard of people who lead deeply religious lives. Let someone begin to spend more time at prayer and less at amusements, let him begin to withdraw from secular pursuits that he might give himself more to God, and there is always the possibility that someone will begin to label him "Jansenistic."

Are Frau Goerres' charges of Jansenism valid,[5] or is it mere witch-hunting on hagiographical levels? To study the charge, we must first search for a definition of terms, and a serviceable and practical definition of Jansenism is given by Pope Pius XI in his *Miserentissimus*:

". . . the most insidious of all heresies, Jansenism, was creeping in, contrary to love and devotion to God, representing Him not as a Father to be loved, but as a merciless judge to be feared."[6] A misrepresentation of God, then, is the root of Jansenism, a distortion which depicts Him as a ruthless judge without a father's mercy; and this culminates in a fearful shrinking away from material things because they could possibly be evil and incur God's wrath. This kind of misguided thinking (or heresy, as the Pope calls it) produces the cold and stiff and unbending attitude which is so characteristic of Jansenism, or any of the other names and forms it has assumed throughout the ages—Puritanism and Albigensianism, to name but two. However this is something entirely different from a valid love of God which attempts to sacrifice material pleasures for His sake, and we must exert extreme care in distinguishing the two in any individual case.

It would appear almost ludicrous to accuse St. Thérèse herself of Jansenism. Her clear concepts of God's mercy are well known, and near the end of her life she made her famous act of oblation to God's *merciful* love. In fact, she insisted so strongly on God's mercy that some of her statements in the autobiography and her letters are embarrassing to professional theologians—as, for example, when she said that God has a poor memory because He cannot remember our faults. And where did she learn these ideas? Pope Pius XII, in his radio address on the occasion of the dedication of the Basilica at Lisieux in 1954, tells us:

As the daughter of a wonderful Christian, she learned at her father's knee the treasures of indulgence and compassion contained in the heart of God.[7]

The very atmosphere of the Martin home was so completely foreign to the cold and stiff attitude of Jansenism: there was warmth, love, humor, and even that cloying sentimentality which many have found difficult to abide. However, the Martins were, as we have noted, exceptionally religious and their deepest values and loyalties rested in spiritual things; the children were taught that the salvation of one's soul is the paramount business of life and that all material things are perishable. It is entirely within the realm of probability that their outlook on life caused them to be called Jansenistic by some of their own neighbors, as well as by later biographers. Such is the peril of a vigorous spiritual life. The important question for us—and it is an important one, since it concerns the education and formation of a saint—is whether or not this religious outlook was authentic and orthodox. Perhaps the best solution, again, is to be found in the official documents of the Holy See and the evaluation they present of the Martins' religious perceptions. In the decree for Thérèse's beatification, Pope Pius XI praised Louis and Zélie Martin for their Christian piety, and in the Bull of Canonization he said:

. . . she was born . . . of religious parents who were remarkable for their outstanding and constant piety.

We are compelled, in a serious pronouncement of this nature, to accept the Pope's words in their precise sense, and if he commends the Martins' piety we must understand "piety" in its accurate meaning of a genuine appreciation and understanding of God's fatherhood. Thus Pope Pius XI sees no evidence of Jansenism in the Martin household; quite to the contrary. In fact, the Popes have always seemed to be impressed with the genuine Christian spirit of the Martin family, and Pope Benedict XV called Louis "a true model of a Christian parent."

The final tribute to the French couple who met accidently on the Pont Saint Leonard that day in 1858 is the fact that serious consideration is now being given to the possibility of canonizing Louis and Zélie Martin.

2. THE YOUNGEST DAUGHTER

Marie Françoise Thérèse Martin was born on the second of January, 1873, in her family's brick and stone home on the Rue Saint Blaise at Alençon, the last of nine children born to Louis and Zélie Martin. Four of the children, two boys and two girls, had died in infancy, leaving only Thérèse's four older sisters—Pauline, Marie, Léonie, and Céline. The young Thérèse was a sickly infant, and the first months of her life were a struggle. In the March following her birth, she almost died, and the decision was made that Thérèse must be breast fed. Since Mme. Martin was unable to feed her children, it was necessary to board the child at the home of a wet nurse, Rose Taille, at Semalle on the outskirts of Alençon. She remained there for a little over a year until Rose's services were no longer needed, returning then to the house at 42, Rue Saint Blaise, the house which today is preserved as a shrine. Reinstated in the family circle, Thérèse grew in that warm and human love for her parents and sisters which has made her so attractive to her devotees.

"I am able to divide my life before I entered Carmel into three periods," Thérèse wrote in the autobiography. "The first, despite its short duration, was by no means the least rich in memories; it begins with the time I attained the use of reason and ends when our dear mother departed for our heavenly home." This was the early childhood of Thérèse, the time she remembers as full of smiles and tenderness. Her mother was still alive, her sisters were doting on her, and her father had conceived a special affection for his youngest daughter. These were the untrammeled years of a pleasant and contented childhood, and Thérèse marks their inception at her attainment of the use of reason.

The age of the use of reason is the stage of a child's life where he begins to distinguish between moral good and evil and to make responsible decisions in that area. In an attempt to gain some workable guide, we usually place that stage at seven years of age, with the understanding that some children attain it earlier, perhaps at the age of five or six, or even younger. Thérèse seems to be one of those children who reach that level of development at a rather early age. At the age of three, we find her making religious decisions and shaping a religious program for herself, and after that there followed an intelligent, responsible pattern such as we associate with a child some six or seven years older. Thérèse herself wrote, "The good God blessed me by opening my intelligence at a very early age," and Pope Pius XI, in the decree for the beatification, said: *She obtained the use of reason when she was barely two years old.*

Before that time, her life appears to have been that of a normal, energetic child. After her return from the wet nurse at Semalle, Thérèse was a healthy, vigorous youngster, rather frolicsome, yet subject to occasional outbursts of temper. Her hair was blond, her eyes what the French call *pers,* an untranslatable word meaning something approaching blue-gray. She had a winning smile which she flashed continually, giving her the pleasant appearance of vivacity and charm. In the autobiography, she recounts the bits of mischief in which she was involved, the pranks, the disagreements with her sisters, her occasional obstinacy. She speaks of herself as being "naughty" and "self-willed," and writes, "You can see, my mother, how far I was from being a child without faults."

Thérèse, then, was not a pious little doll, and these biographers who make her appear so do her a disservice. On the other hand, it would be equally wrong to take very seriously these minor incidents from the life of a spirited child. Thérèse was only two or three at the time, and no great psychological mystery is unraveled when we discover that she lost her temper once in a while, or stamped her foot on the ground, or occasionally failed to do what she was told. She was generally an obedient and docile child, and all these facts must be placed in the total context of her life, facts which show her to be an exuberant and normal youngster.

The religious training implanted by Louis and Zélie Martin in their youngest daughter took early roots and had permanent effects. A few months before her death, Thérèse made an amazing statement to her sister Céline: "From the age of three I have never refused anything to the good God." It is almost an unbelievable statement, one that deserves the most careful consideration, and one that is the key of Thérèse's whole life. There is no evidence of any dramatic decision to live completely for God, nor is there any indication of what at fifteen Thérèse was to call a "conversion." It rather seems that from the dawn of reason she was able, by the grace of God and training she received at home, to make the decision to refuse God nothing she felt He wanted. And the astonishing thing is her success in this resolve! She herself, at the close of her life, said that from the age of three she never did refuse God anything. All the witnesses who testified at the trial said, without exception, that they had never seen her commit a deliberate, willful fault. There were former schoolmates, teachers, priests, confessors, relatives, nuns in her convent—and their testimony was unanimous: she had lived a completely sinless and blameless life.

This is the historical fact with which the biographer must work. One might question the worth of the fact, and say, "Of what value to our age is a little girl who never committed a sin?" Or one might say that Thérèse could then never be of any importance to our weary, sinful world. But this does not change the fact, and some biographers seem reluctant to accept the fact.

In the homily at the canonization Mass, Pius XI said: ". . . and so Thérèse was seen to be of more angelic than human nature." It is a descriptive phrase, one that is particularly interesting since the modern accusation is that the nuns of Lisieux foisted the "angel image" on the world. Actually, it was Pius XI who announced the concept to the world, and it was a concept which, for him, expressed the true historical situation.

Did Thérèse's decision to refuse God nothing change, in any exterior way, the general pattern of her life in that first period? Did she lose her gaiety, become withdrawn, less mischievous? Did she suddenly become an absolutely perfect child, freed from the defects and faults we have observed? The answer to all these questions is no, and it deposits us at one of the most vital questions in Thérèse's life, and in the whole question of sanctity for that matter. She continued to have faults and defects throughout her youth, and even on into her adult years, and perhaps even till her death. These failings disturbed Thérèse, and it was only after she had become a nun that the Franciscan retreat master, Père Alexis, assured her that her faults did not displease God. Thérèse's failings, of course, are what the theologians call "involuntary imperfections," those faults of temper and unkindness and selfishness and moodiness which plague us all our lives. They are faults found in the most spiritual of people, faults which often are blameless in God's sight since they are not committed deliberately or consciously. Thus at the trial Céline stated:

The Servant of God observed all the commandments of God and the precepts of the Church with a perfect exactitude so that no person of my acquaintance ever noticed the least lack of fidelity in this regard. Not only did I fail to see any serious faults in her conduct, but I have never even seen her commit the least voluntary fault.

That would seem to be a definitive and absolute statement, but just a few minutes later Céline added: "Of course Thérèse, especially in her childhood, had small faults; for example, an excessive sensitivity." This might appear to be self-contradictory and confused testimony, but Céline was touching the heart of the matter: Thérèse was blameless in God's sight, but she was not a perfect person, in the absolute sense of the word.

That was Thérèse's lifelong situation: she obtained greater mastery over herself as the years went by, but to the very end she was beset with the weaknesses of our human condition. Her sister Marie recounts an incident which took place in the convent infirmary on July 29, 1897, two months before Thérèse's death. Attempting to provide some diversion for the dying nun, one of the postulants brought her a child's toy (*un petit jouet d'enfant*, Marie called it) and Thérèse accepted it with some astonishment and annoyance. "Now what would I ever do

with that," she asked wearily. The postulant was offended
and told Thérèse that she thought her unkind to make
the remark. "You are right," Thérèse answered, "How
imperfect I am. But I am happy when I experience myself
to be so weak." This was not complacency in her weakness, nor did it express a failure of effort, but merely a
recognition of man's inherent poverty before God. Thérèse refers frequently to this doctrine in her writings and
her instructions to the novices, and it is doctrine we must
examine more carefully later, since it is open to gross misinterpretations.

The amazing fact, however, is that the small girl of
three was able to embark on such a determined program,
and with such generosity and pertinacity, Mme. Martin,
in a letter to Pauline in 1877, comments on this aspect of
her daughter's life:

The other day when she was at the grocery store with
Céline and Louise, she was talking about her religious
practices and discussing them rather loudly with Céline. The lady at the store asked Louise: "What is she
talking about? When she is playing in the garden all
you can hear her discussing are these practices. Mme.
Gaucherin keeps leaning out of her window to try and
learn what it is all about." Our poor little baby is a joy
to all of us, and she will grow up to be a good woman;
you can see the beginnings of it already. She is always
speaking about the good God and would not omit her
prayers for all the world.

But concomitant with her religious fervor, we can also
observe the development of her own individual personality. We see her determined and strong-willed, and Thérèse
herself supplies an example when she tells us how she

grandly refused to kiss the floor one day while her mother
tried to coax her into it by offering her a *sou*. Mme. Martin
comments on this trait in one of her letters:

> She has . . . an almost invincible stubbornness, and
> when she has said "No" nothing can make her give in.
> One could put her in the cellar all day and she would
> remain there all night rather than say "Yes."

We can also observe the usual feminine concern for her
appearance, as when her mother made her wear a long-
sleeved dress on an outing and Thérèse writes: "I let her
dress me with the indifference children that age ought
to have, but interiorly I was thinking how much more
pretty I would have been with bare arms." And we notice
her highly affectionate disposition, fiercely loyal to her
family, eagerly bestowing kisses on her parents and sisters.

Speaking of her sister during these years, Céline said:
"Before the death of my mother, Thérèse was a child full
of warmth, alive, expansive, naturally high-spirited, but
stubborn when it came to the question of displeasing the
Infant Jesus." And Thérèse herself wrote: "Oh, truly the
whole world smiled on me; I found flowers at my feet,
and my happy disposition further contributed to make
my life pleasant."

3. THE FIVE SISTERS

Thérèse's four sisters were all distinct personalities with
their own individual temperaments, and she reacted to
each of them in a different manner. Céline, only four years
her senior, was the closest to her in age, and in many ways

the closest to her in temperament. Céline was lively and frolicsome, and became Thérèse's confidante, playmate, and dear childhood friend. Thérèse preceded Céline into the Carmel by six years, and in a strange reversal, became her older sister's novice mistress. Pauline, eleven and a half years Thérèse's senior, was one of those firm and calm persons of unusual prudence who inspire confidence in the people around them. After the death of their mother, Thérèse chose her as her "Little Mother," and later served under her in the Carmel when Pauline was elected prioress, an office in which Pope Pius XI eventually confirmed her for life. Marie, the eldest sister, thirteen years older than Thérèse, was of an active, extremely practical disposition. During Mme. Martin's final illness and after her death, Marie actually ran the household, making the purchases, arranging for the meals, and supervising the welfare of the family. She ultimately became procuratrix (treasurer and buyer) in the Carmel, an office perfectly suited to her temperament. Thérèse confessed that she would actually have chosen Marie as her "Little Mother," but Céline chose her first, and Thérèse then turned to Pauline so as not to offend her.

The middle daughter, Léonie, nine and a half years older than Thérèse, presented somewhat of a problem for Louis and Zélie Martin, and she apparently presents something of a problem for modern biographers, too. Frau Goerres depicts her in the role of a French Cinderella: a person of genuine quality who is misunderstood by the family, an object of embarrassment and intolerance.[8] Goerres contends that the reason for Léonie's unpopularity with the family was her refusal to accept the prevalent bourgeois concept of religion. In actuality, Léonie was a problem child—and she herself freely admitted this—for the invariable reasons that some children have always been problems; she was sulky at home, often disobedient to her parents, and found it hard to get along with outsiders because of her irascible temperament. The Martins twice placed her in the Visitation school at Le Mans, but the nuns sent her home each time because she became unruly and obstreperous and was unable to keep up with the other children in scholastic work. (Goerres, incidentally, states that the Martins sent Léonie to Le Mans to rid themselves of her. However, Pauline and Marie attended Le Mans, too, and were withdrawn hurriedly by their father when the Germans began to march on the city in 1870.) As she grew older, there was a marked amelioration in Léonie's condition, and she eventually decided to become a nun. But even then her problem of adjustment asserted itself. In 1886, acting on a sudden impulse, she joined the Poor Clares in Alençon, but left after a few weeks. Later she joined the Visitation nuns, but twice more she failed to persevere, and only after Thérèse's death did she enter and remain in the Visitation convent.

Our only concern with Léonie's problem is the manner in which this influenced her relationship with Thérèse, although we might state that the rest of the family was entirely sympathetic with Léonie, treated her with love and compassion, and made no attempt to exclude her from the family circle. At the trial, Léonie asserted that Thérèse was always extremely kind toward her:

She was truly the joy of the family. The servants loved her very much because everything within her reflected peace, kindness and sympathy. She was continually forgetful of herself, trying to give happiness to others . . . She went to great pains not to humiliate or sadden anybody. I noticed that very especially in a personal situation of mine. When I was twenty-three years of age I was very much retarded in my spelling and my studies, having had great difficulties in learning. Thérèse, who was about ten years younger than I, worked very hard to help me fill in the gaps in my education. As she was doing this, I admired the delicacy and unalterable patience she possessed in rendering me this service without embarrassing me in any way at all.

Thérèse remained concerned about Léonie all her life, and during her final illness she said she would pray for her assiduously in heaven. Thérèse's last letter to her was dated July 17, 1897, and in it she wrote:

In heaven you want me to pray to the Sacred Heart for you; rest assured that I shall not forget to give Him your messages or ask Him for all that is necessary for you to become a great saint. Goodbye, dearest sister, I want the thought of my entry into heaven to fill you with joy, for there I can love you still better.

And Léonie always maintained that she owed her success in the religious life to the prayers of her young sister in heaven.

Another aspect of Thérèse's relationship to her family is worthy of consideration: the charge, frequently made by the critics, that Thérèse was a spoiled child. This is not a new charge—in fact, it was made thirty years ago in Henri Ghéon's study of Thérèse when he titled a chapter of his book *Secret of the Little Flower*, "The Spoilt Child"—and it is one that a cursory reading of the evidence might appear to substantiate. Thérèse was undoubtedly the favorite of her father; she herself admits that, and all the witnesses at the trial testify to it. She was his "little queen" whom he petted, took on walks with him, and upon whom he lavished his special attention. Thérèse was more prettily dressed than the other daughters, and she was the only one whose hair was curled, simply because M. Martin liked it that way. Thérèse writes of Sunday at home in language that corresponds alarmingly to that of a spoiled child:

> From the very beginning I remained in bed longer that day than usual, and Pauline spoiled her little child by bringing her chocolate in bed and then dressing her like a princess. Marie curled the hair of her godchild, and I was not very pleasant when she combed it roughly.

These facts, and many others, have led some biographers to make a quick conclusion that Thérèse Martin must inevitably have been a very spoiled little youngster. Father Robo, for example, speaking of Thérèse's own protestation that she was not spoiled, writes:

> Even some of her simplest affirmations cannot be accepted literally; for instance when she says, "My father did not spoil me," though on her own evidence it is perfectly clear that he did. Not only was her old father incapable of disagreeing with her, but in this household, a French household in 1887–1888, Teresa, a big girl of twelve, thirteen, fourteen, did not take her share of housework. She did not even make her own bed. Her sisters did it for her, and like a little princess, Teresa did not wait upon herself. When Teresa says, "I was not spoilt," we are entitled to disagree. (p. 61)

Father Robo is denying St. Thérèse's own evaluation of her education at home, for in the section of the autobiography addressed to her sister Pauline, she writes:

I have asked myself many times how you were able to
bring me up with so much love and tenderness and
yet without spoiling me. You certainly never allowed
any imperfection of mine to escape, and every reproach
of yours was truly deserved. You never retreated on any
of your decisions after you had made them, and I was
so well aware of it that I would not have been able to
take a step if you had forbidden it.

The witnesses at the trial are in complete harmony that
Thérèse was not spoiled, despite a home situation which
would have made it very easy. The ecclesiastical judges
who conducted the trial were keenly aware of the possibility, and we find them frequently interrupting the
testimony to ask the pointed question: "Was Thérèse a
spoiled child?" All the responses were in the vein of the
testimony given by Père Pichon, the Jesuit, who stated
that some other child could have become spoiled in such
a situation, radically affecting her development, but it
was not the case with Thérèse Martin. Léonie said:

It is quite evident that Thérèse was the object of an
entirely special affection both on the part of my father
and on the part of my mother, during the few years
she lived. But we were not jealous. On the contrary,
we too had a special affection for our little sister. She
was the "Benjamin" of the whole family. She was such
a charming infant. And, on her part, Thérèse did not
in the least abuse this special affection; she was as obedient as the rest of us, even more so, and I never
noticed any kind of superior attitude towards the rest
of us.

Some of the witnesses recounted specific incidents to
illustrate their point, as did Céline, recalling an episode

involving the morning newspaper. Each morning when
the newspaper arrived—*Le Croix*, the Royalist newspaper
published every evening in Paris and delivered to the
provinces in the morning—Thérèse liked to carry it upstairs to her father. One day Céline wanted to perform
this service for her father, but Thérèse as usual had managed to gain possession of the newspaper first. An animated discussion ensued between the two girls, but Thérèse refused to relinquish the paper and Céline dispiritedly
conceded. However M. Martin overheard the discussion
and reprimanded Thérèse for her lack of consideration to
her sister. M. Martin scolded her so severely, in fact, that
Céline said she felt miserable about the whole episode.

Pauline remembered that, after the death of his wife,
M. Martin was even more careful about his *petite reine*
in this regard. Pauline had complete charge of the young
girl during that time and she said:

> I never saw her disobedient; she asked permission for
> everything. When our father asked her to go out for a
> walk with him, she always responded: "I must go and
> ask permission from Pauline." My father agreed to this
> arrangement, and if I refused permission, she obeyed
> without insisting, although she did cry sometimes be-
> cause she knew how much my father liked to walk with
> her.

This is illuminating testimony about the question at
hand, and Thérèse herself recounts the same facts in her
autobiography. The significance of the testimony becomes
apparent when we consider what a spoiled child would
have done in similar circumstances; a child who was
spoiled, a special favorite of her father, yet placed under
the care of an older sister, would assuredly have played
off the sister against the father, running from one to the

other, seeking to have her sister's orders rescinded by her father. That she did not do it seems compelling evidence that we are not dealing with a spoiled child.

Some of the most intriguing testimony in the whole *Processus* is given by one Marceline Husé, whom Thérèse encountered at a later stage in her life after the family moved from Alençon to Lisieux. Marceline was a country girl brought into service at the home of Thérèse's uncle, Isidore Guérin. She was only a few years older than Thérèse, and performed service which we might approximate to that of a chambermaid, but because of the close association between the two families she had frequent contact with Thérèse: taking her on walks, chaperoning her, occasionally serving her meals. Thérèse was always kind to the girl in service, especially at the beginning of their association when she consoled her in the homesickness she experienced working in the Guérin household. Speaking about Thérèse in the present matter, Marceline said:

> Since she was the youngest, she received special affection, which however in no way contradicted her splendid upbringing. He [M. Martin] did not allow her to get away with anything at all. I am not sure if little Thérèse, who was so humble, realized that she was the best loved, for in that family there was a tremendous union of hearts. At any rate, she was not a spoiled child, and she did nothing to take advantage of her position.

There is an abundance of testimony by Marceline stating her admiration and respect for the little girl she had to serve. If Carlyle could state that no man is a hero to his own valet, we can at least point to a case where a small girl was a heroine to her servant.

Much more evidence could be cited, but it all repetitiously emphasizes the same point: Thérèse was not spoiled. A concise summation of this question is given by John Beevers in his fine and perceptive book, *Storm of Glory*:

> To sum up: Thérèse could have been spoilt. The conditions for it were there. She nearly was, but on the evidence of her relatives, her associates, her confessors and, completely conclusive, on the evidence of her life in Carmel, she was not.[9]

One final point might interest us, as it interested the judges at the trial when they asked Pauline why Thérèse was the favorite of her father. Her answer:

> She was the youngest child, and she was also particularly intelligent and affectionate. She understood my father's heart completely, and he found his consolation in her after our mother's death.

4. THE END OF SPRINGTIME

Zélie Martin had apparently been harrassed by the symptoms of cancer for a number of years, but when she finally approached the doctor she was informed that it was then inoperable. She accepted her fate calmly, made preparations for her death, and grew gradually weaker and more enfeebled as the cancer spread. The swelling in her breast developed, and then another tumor appeared in her neck, and finally a fibrous swelling on her back. At Christmas of 1876, she received Extreme Unction, but revived enough to make a pilgrimage to Lourdes in the following June with the three oldest girls. The trip was a difficult one, and Mme. Martin encountered a series of contretemps in travel, accommodations, and meals. She bathed a number of times in the icy water at the Piscine, prayed at the Grotto, but it soon became evident that she would not be the recipient of a miracle. On her return to Alençon, she wrote to her brother:

> Tell me, could we possibly have had a more unfortunate journey? To be sure, there were great graces, and those will amply compensate me for all the discomforts. . . . The Blessed Virgin has said to us as she said to Bernadette: "I do not promise to make you happy in this world but in the next."[10]

The young girls, stunned at the failure to receive a miraculous cure, set themselves to the grim task of watching their mother die. Zélie attempted to remain active as long as she could, and the girls recalled hearing her groan and whimper in pain each evening in her room. Finally she was committed to bed, and in the last stages of the illness Thérèse and Céline were taken to a neighbor's house during the daytime. On the twenty-eighth of August, 1877, she expired. She was only forty-six years old.

Mme. Martin died near midnight, and Thérèse was not informed of it until the following morning. Her father lifted her up to kiss the forehead of her deceased mother, and Thérèse later wrote: "I do not recall that I cried very much, and I could not speak to anybody about what I was feeling in my heart." The child was treated with all the courtesies and sympathies usually extended to a young girl who has lost her mother, but no one seemed to realize what profound and lasting effects Mme. Martin's death was to have on Thérèse. She was then four years and eight months old, and she was at the start of a new epoch in her life. She wrote:

A new period of my life was beginning for me. I had to endure the trial of fire, and to suffer from my youth so as to prove my love for Jesus. Just as the spring flowers begin to germinate under the snow before they can bud forth under the sun's rays, so too the little flower whose story I am writing had to endure the winter of trial.

A few months after his wife's death, M. Martin moved the family to Lisieux. One of the principal attractions of Lisieux was the presence of the Guérin family, Mme. Martin's relatives. M. Martin felt that Mme. Guérin could help him in raising his five daughters. The Martin family rented a pleasant red-brick, three-story home in a quiet section of the parish of Saint Jacques; the house, with its neat English garden, has since become known throughout the world as Les Buissonnets, the name given it by the Martin girls because of its two gardens and its maze of bushes and shrubbery. It was at Les Buissonnets that the principal childhood recollections St. Thérèse recounts in her autobiography took place. Thérèse became devoted to her aunt and uncle and their two children, Jeanne and Marie. Marie Guérin (whom M. Martin always called "the Greek girl," because of her darting black eyes) was three years older than Thérèse, and the two girls became close friends.

The Martin family began its readjustment at Lisieux, and the general pattern was the same as before Mme. Martin died. Marie took over the management of the house, Pauline assumed the special care of Thérèse, and M. Martin, now retired from business, was able to give more time to his family. Thérèse began to accompany her father to the six o'clock Mass each morning at St. Pierre, and in the afternoons the two of them would go for a walk.

There was the usual game of draughts in the evening, followed by the reading aloud, and M. Martin, his face creased in smiles, could be seen joggling his youngest daughter on his knee. But it soon became evident that a radical change had occurred in Thérèse. She herself describes it:

> . . . after Mamma's death my happy disposition changed completely. I who had been so lively and so expansive, now became timid and shy and extremely sensitive. I could be plunged into tears by a look, and I was quite happy to be left alone by everybody. I could not endure the company of strangers, and I only recovered my gaiety when I was alone with the family.

Her sister, Céline, commented on Thérèse's change of character:

> After the death of my mother, the happy character of Thérèse changed, and she was no longer cheerful. . . . The most serious defect of this epoch of her life was her excessive sensitiveness: she cried at the least thing, and when she had finished crying, she cried for having cried. And she was aware that all of this was a great weakness. . . . Outside the family circle at Les Buissonnets she was excessively timid. She liked to keep herself hidden, believing herself inferior to everybody else. But in our company, and only there, she regained her gaiety and expansiveness.

The loss of her mother, therefore, was a profound shock to the affectionate little girl, and ten years would pass before she recovered from it. These were the years Thérèse called her "martyrdom," years of weariness and

dissatisfaction. The springtime of life had terminated for
her, and the world was now a more grim and harsh place.
She became quiet and reflective, and things upset her
easily. She could be wounded more quickly, and she cried
frequently. Yet despite all of this she did not become a
difficult person; her temperamental problems were with
herself and not those around her. She continued her determined religious program: prayer, daily attendance at
Mass, acts of charity, the constant little sacrifices she so
carefully tabulated—in a word, a generous attempt to
please God in all things. There is no record of any irascibility or anger on her part, no emotional outbursts or
touchiness that made it difficult for people to approach
her. When Thérèse uses the word "sensitive," it can only
mean, as we test it against the other evidence and the
statements of the witnesses, that she had become emo-
tionally delicate, prone to tears, downcast more readily,
and weary of life. She struggled against any external
manifestation of her problem, but that, of course, was
impossible: her tears were noticed, and Marceline Husé
speaks of how Thérèse's face would flush as she tried to
overcome herself. The witnesses remark on her continuing
kindness during this period, her desire to offend no one,
and her delicacy in dealing even with the servants. She
was as docile and obedient as before, and she unhesitatingly did what she was told. Her problem was herself
as she tried to live on in a world which had been cruelly
ripped apart by her mother's death.

In her autobiography, Thérèse records the details of
life at Les Buissonnets. There are stories of her fishing
trips with her father, her games with Céline and Marie
Guérin, her visits to church. They are simple and usual
stories of a child's life, but there is one episode which is
as mystifying as it is unusual: Thérèse's childhood ap-

parition. One day when her father was away on a trip, she was looking out on the garden from an upstairs window and saw a man whom she thought to be her father walking toward the bushes. He had the same gait, dress, and general appearance as her father, but his head was draped in a thick veil. It was a disturbing sight, and Thérèse cried out to the man, but he had strangely disappeared. Her sisters heard her calling and rushed to her, and when she tried to tell them that she had seen her father in the garden, they explained that he was away and not due back for several days. Thérèse interpreted this in her autobiography as a prophetic vision of her father's future illness. It is difficult to classify this incident with any degree of certainty, and there have been some varying opinions on it. But it is interesting to note that the official documents of the Holy See pay scant attention to this episode, preferring not to make any decision about it.

There are only a few similar incidents in Thérèse's life, and their very absence highlights another important aspect of her life, perhaps the most important and valuable of all. Thérèse was a saint of the ordinary, and there is a singular lack of the sensational, of the extraordinary, in it. As one of the witnesses at the trial commented, she became a saint by doing ordinary things extraordinarily well. And by living an ordinary, almost monotonous life, she calls our attention to the essence of sanctity. She disabuses us of the idea that sanctity consists in the performance of outstanding feats of endurance or accomplishment. She reminds us that sanctity is basically a relationship with God in which we love Him, do His will, become concerned with His glory. She stated: "Sanctity does not consist in this or that practice, but rather in a disposition of the heart which makes us humble and small

in the arms of God." Pope Pius XI, in the Bull of Canonization, called special attention to this when he stated
that Thérèse's particular kind of sanctity consisted in
readily, generously, and constantly fulfilling her vocation
without going beyond the common order of things (*quin
communem ordinem excesserit*). The phrase is of tremendous value in understanding her gift to the Church,
and the reason, perhaps, that the Popes have so frequently
proposed her for our imitation.

Without going beyond the common order of things.
This is a kind of leitmotiv running through her life, a
theme that presents itself at every stage of her short
twenty-four years. There is in her life no adventure, no
excitement, no romance, no drama—at least not in the
commonly accepted sense of those words. She is not like
a St. Vincent de Paul climbing through the alleys of
Paris with his bandages and loaves of bread; nor like a St.
John of the Cross, stripped to the waist, being lashed in
the monastery at Toledo; nor like a St. Joan of Arc raising
the siege at Orleans and ultimately writhing in pain as
she was burned at the stake. Thérèse is not even like so
many nun-saints: she does not resemble St. Jane Frances
de Chantal, who literally had to step over her own children as she left home to follow God's call; nor does she
resemble St. Teresa of Avila, who had to rattle all over
Spain in a covered wagon founding convents. Instead,
Thérèse is a charming, shy little girl from the provinces
who played checkers, had a pet dog named Tom, liked
snowflakes and flowers, a girl who was the object of much
affection and sympathy, who entered a local convent and
died a few years later. She had no family opposition to her
entering the convent; rather, her father himself took her
to the convent door. She did not die in a strange land,
surrounded by strangers, as did St. Francis Xavier on the
island of Sanchen off the China coast; rather, she died,

propped up in a clean bed, attended by her own devoted sisters. This is not the stuff of adventure or drama.
It is only the rather ordinary and unexciting tale of a
common little life. But in the framework of that life she
became a saint, and therein lies the genius of her message: she teaches us to become saints in the framework
of *our* lives. And are not our lives, for the most part, composed of routine and unspectacular elements?

If anyone would look to a spectacular hero for inspiration, he will not find it in Thérèse Martin. But if he would
discover how to become a saint while involved in the
drama of day-to-day, depressing, commonplace routine,
then Thérèse can enlighten him immeasurably. Thérèse's
simple and unexciting life has proved unattractive to
some readers, despite the fact that the modern Popes
have so consistently asked us to study her, and one can
only wonder what one is seeking in the life of a saint.
An ecclesiastical adventure story? An Horatio Alger tale
in a cassock? Or is one looking for an answer to that
vital question: How can I become a saint, too? If so, Thérèse can supply an answer to that question.

The Martin home in Lisieux, Les Buissonnets, is now a
pilgrimage site, and each year thousands of pilgrims file
past a huge relic cabinet in Thérèse's former bedroom on
the second floor. On display in the cabinet are a variety of
articles she used in her childhood: a toy stove, a skipping
rope, a checkerboard, a sailboat, her schoolbooks. So
often the visitors smile as they study these relics of an
ordinary childhood, and a look of understanding flashes
into their eyes. Anyone who has visited the home of another nineteenth-century French saint, St. Bernadette's
house in Lourdes, is immediately struck by the sharp contrast. Bernadette's family was from a much lower income
group, and her home is a dark and forbidding place hidden beneath the street level in one of the more unattrac-

tive sections of Lourdes. Here the visitor can be awed as he witnesses the poverty-stricken hovel of a saint who was to see the Virgin in the cave at Massiabielle and whose whole life was to be crossed with misunderstandings and opposition; and here, once again, we are involved in the dramatic. None of that is present at Lisieux. There we have only a charming Norman country house, and the pleasant remembrances of a comfortable childhood, some books and some pink-cheeked dolls. But the visitor can almost be heard to say, "I know this girl. I understand her. She is within the world of my experience."

This is what Thérèse has done: she has brought sanctity into focus; she has made it comprehensible to us in terms of a life we know and understand and experience. That is her accomplishment.

5. "I REFUSED THE GOOD GOD NOTHING"

When Thérèse was approaching her seventh birthday she made her first confession at the Cathedral Church of St. Pierre, and she continued to make frequent confessions, despite the fact that, in accordance with the custom of the time, she did not receive her first Communion until she was eleven years old. One of her early confessors, Abbé Domin, the chaplain at the Benedictine Abbey School, testified at the trial about his young penitent:

As a confessor, I am following the procedure used in the process of canonization of St. Aloyisius Gonzaga, and I believe I am free to say that my impression today is that during that time of her life the Servant of God never committed a completely deliberate fault.

This is the fact that must be retained in mind as we study the comfortable childhood of Thérèse and witness her struggling with her own internal problems: she was still adamant in her resolve to refuse the good God nothing. She was a child, but her religious instincts and motivation were mature and solid. Marceline Husé said at the trial:

> She was a soul who lived continually in the presence of God, for if you spoke to her of clothes or fashions or anything of that kind, you could not continue the conversation for long. But if I spoke to her about religious things, all at once her soul opened up and her heart expanded with happiness.

Marie, her sister, engaged Thérèse in a conversation about her attachment to God:

> How are you always able to think of God?

> It is not difficult. One naturally thinks about what one loves.

> Then you never lose the presence of God?

> Oh no, I believe that I have never spent more than three minutes without thinking of God.

Thérèse had unusually clear religious concepts. Religion, for her, was not only a moral code to be followed; it was, more basically, a relationship with God, an adventure in friendship with Him. She called God *Papa le bon Dieu*, a phrase she developed in her childhood, and even used occasionally in her later life. God, therefore, was not distant figure in the sky with a flowing gray beard, as He is for so many children, but rather He was her Father, Someone to know and Someone to love.

Anyone who has read Thérèse's autobiography, or her letters, might be forced to the conclusion that her approach to religion was a sentimental one. There is talk of harts and does, snowflakes, and spring flowers; curly little lambs and chirping birds are used to illustrate points; and there is a constant discussion of giving pleasure to the little Infant Jesus, even becoming His little plaything if necessary. However, we must not let this cant, this unbearable mode of expression, obfuscate and becloud Thérèse's basic religious concepts. The deeper we probe into her life, the more we see that, while her language might have been sentimental, her religion was not. Marceline Husé records a conversation she had with the young Thérèse about loving God:

> She explained to me that love does not consist in sentiment, but in the practice of virtue, and it is necessary to seek always to please the good God in all our actions without trying to attract any attention.

This concept remained clear in her mind throughout her life, and years later in the convent her sister Pauline questioned her as to why she was placing flowers around the stone crucifix in the middle of the cloister garden.

> Are you trying to obtain some grace?

> No, it is only to give Him pleasure. I do not want to give for the purpose of receiving. I am not an egoist; it is the good God and not myself that I love.

Thérèse, therefore, had a fine perception of what loving God meant and entailed. She understood that, while we must love God as a person and become fascinated by

Him, this love is proved by service, by deeds; and she knew, even as a very young child, that this love is proved, tested, and augmented by suffering. But her written expression of these mature concepts can generate fears in some minds that we are dealing with a pietistic, sentimental, and puerile brand of religion. Nothing could be further from the truth. Thérèse was rooted in the most authentic traditions of Christian spirituality: Pope Pius XI said that she nourished her soul by a continual reading of the Scriptures, and she obtained her ascetical doctrine from the *Imitation of Christ*, and her mystical doctrine from the works of St. John of the Cross. There is a world of difference, though, between the terse phrases of the *Imitation* or the uncompromising truths of St. John of the Cross and the honeyed pages of St. Thérèse—but the difference is only on the verbal level, not on the conceptual level. Her perceptions were orthodox, but her style and her writing represented the very worst of the late Romantic period. Late Romanticism in art and writing has now happily passed away, although it seems to flourish in some areas of Catholic art and statuary, but Thérèse lived in the full stream of that movement. It was a period when artists busied themselves in depicting cherubs and cupids, when decorating was oppressively overdone, when writing became effusive and fulsome, when artistic bad taste abounded. Thérèse's environment produced her literary style, and even her spoken expression.

No apology need be made for Thérèse's mincing, callow style. It was poor style, a product of one of the very worst artistic eras in the world's history. But through this argot Thérèse expressed herself, and we must not confine her to style and vocabulary. It is not so much *how* she said it, but rather *what* she said. Thérèse was an astonishingly honest person, and she meant every word she wrote. When she uses what we might now term a cliché (if that word has any meaning at all, since all lasting and endurable expressions must eventually become clichés) we must remember that it was not a cliché or a mere verbalism for her. Every word, every phrase, was deeply felt and experienced. Her articulation was limited to the mode of that time, but in those clumsy and awkward expressions she was trying to express the most vital truths with all the honesty, all the candor she could muster.

Jean Guitton, a member of the French Academy, feels that we must accept Thérèse's style at face value as an honest attempt to express her thought. In his rewarding little book, *The Spiritual Genius of St. Thérèse,* he says:

> Thérèse will give a new value to the word. Whatever she says, she does, and her sayings are like oracles. I say her sayings: I distinguish them from her language. Thérèse's language is imperfect on account of the weakness of the human beings who transmitted a very second-rate tongue to her . . . As a result, wherever Thérèse followed the bad taste of her time, she alone was not in bad taste: for a style is always good when it is exact and true.[11]

Although Thérèse's style has repelled many, it must be admitted that it has also attracted many, and a good deal of the initial enthusiasm for her was generated by the sweet and sometimes sentimental phraseology she employed. This had both desirable and undesirable results: desirable, when people who ordinarily would not have read St. John of the Cross or St. Teresa of Avila were easily introduced to the staggering Christian truths she so gently taught; undesirable, when people identified vocabulary with doctrine and were deluded into believing that Thérèse was proposing a soft and sentimental road to heaven. Fortunately, later studies attempted to point out the relationship of language to concept; and recently Msgr. Knox translated her autobiography in modern idiom, deleting the Gallicisms and expressions of her age.

St. Thérèse was pious, in the best sense of that word; but she was not pietistic, in the pejorative sense of the word. Piety is a true virtue, or perhaps better, a grouping of virtues which makes us recognize the fatherhood of God and respond to Him in a filial manner. The state of being pietistic, if we may attribute a definition to it for our own purposes here, consists in sentimentalizing about religion and affecting a religious pose. Thérèse was far removed from that latter state. She was a realist where religion was concerned. Pauline said about her:

> She detested the little devotions of pious women (*les petites devotions de bonne femme*) which were sometimes introduced into the convent. Collections of prayers gave her a headache; she said that the Divine Office, the Pater, and the Ave were enough to move her heart.

This is a hardheaded and realistic approach to religion, quite different from the impression that we receive of her when we read the pretty phrases of the autobiography. But if we are to discover the real Thérèse, and if we are to learn anything valuable from her, we must look at the determined little girl who refused God nothing, who endured her "winter of trial," who wanted to love God without reward. Thérèse is like Nora in Ibsen's *A Doll's House:* in our first impressions of her we might imagine her to be a rather shallow, insipid person, but as we grow in knowledge of her we recognize her depth of character, her firmness.

6. LA DEMI-PENSIONNAIRE

In October, 1881, when she was eight years old, Thé-rèse began to attend classes at the Benedictine abbey in Lisieux. The abbey, which was later completely destroyed by Allied bombers during the Second World War, was a typical French convent school with well-scrubbed little girls and imperturbable nuns. A quick and clever student, she was placed in a class of girls older than herself, and this, plus her own shyness, made her career at school rather unpleasant for her. Thérèse confessed frankly that she detested school life at the convent:

> I have often heard it said that school days are the best and happiest time of one's life. That was not true in my case. The five years I spent there were the saddest of my whole life.

Thérèse was only a day student (*une demi-pensionnaire*) at the convent, returning home late every afternoon. She went to and from school in the company of her sister Céline and her cousin Marie Guérin, and Thérèse admitted that only Céline's presence made school bearable. There have been other children in the history of the world who found school unattractive, and the contention of some critics that this constituted a serious abnormality would seem to be unrealistic.

One of the reasons for Thérèse's adverse reaction to life at the abbey was her own temperament—affectionate, and now timid and shy since the death of her mother—which made the stiff and regimented life of the convent unpleasant for her. She had grown up in the surroundings of a warm and tender family life, and the whitewashed walls and marching children in the convent constituted an abrupt and unsatisfactory change. Céline did not share the same sentiments, but then Thérèse was of a much more delicate and affectionate temperament. The differing reactions of Thérèse and Céline are part of the story of life: one child likes school, and another does not.

Thérèse became an outsider at the abbey in one important facet of school life: she did not participate in the athletic games. Céline states that her sister tried to participate but was unable to do so because of an alarming shortness of breath—and we must remember that Thérèse died at only twenty-four of a pulmonary ailment.

She was an above-average student, her favorite subjects being history and French composition. Mathematics she found uninteresting. Céline tells us that she studied diligently but preferred rather to get the sense of the material than a word-for-word memorization. Before starting school, she had been tutored at home by her sisters, thus she was able to skip a few grades at the abbey. She was only eight, but she was placed in a class in which some of the girls were as old as thirteen or fourteen, and even then she led her class in studies. Sister St. Francis de Sales, one of her teachers, testified at the trial that Thérèse often asked questions with a depth that embarrassed her, questions about God's mercy and human liberty. Her teacher remembers that when Thérèse was about nine she found it difficult to accept the doctrine that infants dying without baptism are deprived of God's vision.

Abbé Domin, who taught catechism to the girls, was so impressed with her sharp mind that he called her "his little doctor." Thérèse herself records an incident with the Abbé:

One time the girl who followed me could not remember the question to ask the next student. The Abbé asked all the students without success, then returned to me and said he would see if I deserved my place at the head of the class. In my profound humility I was just waiting for that! I rose calmly, and answered the question perfectly to the astonishment of the rest of the class.

The episode is interesting because it demonstrates her ability at school work, but also because it shows us Thérèse indulging in a bit of gentle irony at her own expense. In the abbey school the students had to memorize the catechism question as well as the answer, and when the girl behind her stumbled on a question Thérèse had to wait for all the other girls to be interrogated before her turn came again. Thérèse knew the question and was impatiently waiting for her turn to come so that she could demonstrate her knowledge. For this reason she chides herself in the autobiography, "In my profound humility I was just waiting for that"; and she underlines the phrase "In my profound humility" heavily in the manuscript. Father Robo recounts the incident, but misinterprets it completely:

"In my profound humility, I waited (to be questioned) and, standing with great assurance, I answered without making . . ." What had her profound humility to do with this, one may wonder!

Father Robo's inaccurate and humorless reading of the text reveals, perhaps more than any careful textual criticism, the solemn and ponderous metality of the new critics as they study Thérèse's life.

The Papal documents make reference to Thérèse's intellectual prowess; for example, in the brief for the beatification:

Her intelligence was far in advance of her age and she had great success in her studies, especially history. She had a keen memory, and memorized the entire *Imitation of Christ*.

Her scholastic successes, however, were not always appreciated by her fellow students, as so often happens in the small world of the classroom. She was a younger girl in a class of older girls, yet she surpassed all of them scholastically; and here we have a timeless setting for petty schoolgirl jealousies. While the testimony at the trial shows that Thérèse was liked and respected at the school, there were still a number of girls who did not care for the shy little girl who was so brilliant at studies, who did not participate in their games, and who spent a considerable amount of time praying in the chapel. Marguerite Leroy, a student at the abbey during Thérèse's time, recalls that, "She seemed timid and extremely sensitive, but with a sweet and likable cheerfulness." But Céline remembers that Thérèse suffered while at school at the hands of some "country students" who did not share her tastes or aspirations, and Marie says that she was hurt by some of the girls who were rather coarse (*une nature plus vulgaire*). We might suspect some hauteur on the part of the Martin girls, but one of the teachers, Sister St. Francis de Sales, confirms their testimony, citing the case of a girl in the abbey who submitted Thérèse to a *petite persecution*. The girl, Sister Francis said, had an odd personality and became very much opposed to Thérèse, and although the girl took pains to embarrass Thérèse, none of the sisters could remember her complaining or asking for redress.

The student, Marguerite Leroy, was asked to give her opinion why Thérèse was unhappy at school, and she answered:

I think I can give the reason why. It was the sharp contrast she experienced between, on the one hand, the warmth of her own family milieu with its deep piety, and on the other, the composition of the Abbey School which at that time contained a certain number of somewhat coarse pupils.

Sister Francis also remembers that one of the pupils was from a poor family, and she herself shabby and unattractive, but Thérèse went out of her way to engage her in conversation and be kind to her. "I am convinced," the teacher said, "that in her solicitude for that student there was no natural attraction of any kind; Thérèse was motivated by fraternal charity and the good of the child's soul."

She found blessed relief from life at the abbey in the evenings at home, the Thursday holiday, and especially on Sundays. On Sunday, she attended high Mass with her father, then played with her sister Céline, and went on a longer walk with her father in the afternoon. In the late afternoon, she returned to church for Compline services, and as the shadows lengthened she was brought face to face with the unwelcome fact that a new week of school would begin in a few hours. She writes:

But I must return to our Sundays again. That joyous day passed so quickly, leaving a strain of melancholy at the end. I remember that my happiness was undiminished up to the time of Compline; and during the Office I thought to myself that the day of rest is soon coming to an end and on the morrow I must begin life again, working, learning my lessons. It was then that I really felt that this earth was an exile, and I yearned for the eternal rest of heaven, the place where every day is Sunday in our true home.

The only durable contact she had outside her home and the abbey was the Guérin household. Jeanne Guérin was five years older than Thérèse, and at the trial remarked, justly, that five years are a big difference to the young and thus she and Thérèse were never really companions. Marie, however, did become a close friend of the future saint, and Thérèse recounts a number of their mutual childhood episodes in the autobiography. The two girls picked flowers together, played games, and pretended they were hermits in one of the small sheds behind the house. Thérèse recalls the incident when the two of them decided to walk along the sidewalk with their eyes tightly closed; they maneuvered along successfully for several minutes, then at the same time they both stumbled over a stand outside a store, upsetting the contents on the pavement. The enraged shopkeeper emerged to retrieve his merchandise and began shouting at the two girls while they sped down the street, their eyes now fully open.

Marie Guérin, however, at this stage of her life, tended to be a difficult and inconsiderate person. Marceline Husé testified that she was often sick and made frequent and capricious demands, which Thérèse tried to fulfill cheerfully and quickly. "What acts of patience she performed towards her!" Marceline said. Léonie recalls that one day Thérèse called her aunt "Mamma," and Marie Guérin tartly informed her that Mme. Guérin was not her mother and that she did not have any mother. Léonie saw the tears form in Thérèse's eyes, but she made no reply to her cousin and continued to treat her as kindly as before.

Jeanne Guérin, the older of Thérèse's two cousins, testified at the trial about the little girl who used to play in their home:

At that time I was certainly far from thinking that one day she would be working miracles as she is doing to-

day and being discussed all over the world. But as far
as her virtues are concerned, I believe that, during
the years we lived near each other, her virtue was completely extraordinary and surpassed even what you
observe in the most virtuous persons.

The judges at the trial tried to make Jeanne Guérin
testify a little more precisely, and asked her if she could
mention some specific virtues. Jeanne responded:

I never saw her do anything extraordinary, but what
seemed heroic in her conduct was that her virtue never
wavered, even in those childhood years of which I am
speaking. She was remarkable, above all, for her humility, her obedience, her kindness, and her charity
towards her neighbor.

Jeanne Guérin, therefore, touches the same theme that
Pope Pius XI articulated: Thérèse was remarkably holy
without going beyond the common order of things.

In attempting to fashion a portrait of Thérèse during
her childhood years, a portrait which corresponds with
the factual situation, we must not omit one aspect of her
personality which is mentioned in the Papal documents.
Speaking of the time immediately after the death of her
mother, Pope Benedict XV says:

. . . the death of her mother produced in her a seriousness and maturity of mind far in advance of her
years. . . . It is certain that from this time Thérèse
furnished proof of an extraordinary maturity of judgment, both in her words and deeds.

The Pope speaks of her extraordinary maturity, something that would hardly seem compatible with Thérèse's

emotional problems, her tears, her sensitivity. And the witnesses at the trial also talk about her maturity, for example, Léonie, who said, "She had a maturity superior to her age." If we are to accept the testimony of the witnesses and the statement of the Pope it means that we must see Thérèse's emotional problems in the character of a basically mature person; it means that her difficulties were not as debilitating or incapacitating as we might first believe; it means that some latter-day critics have distorted Thérèse's problems out of context and blown them up into abnormalities.

Thérèse cried easily. The world was a grim and cheerless place after her mother's death. She became shy, timid, preferred the company of her family. But are these serious abnormalities—expecially when we consider that she made sound, mature judgments, that she had basic control of herself, that she was said to have a maturity "superior to her age"?

While some biographers see Thérèse's childhood problems as a study of developing abnormality, she herself did not view them in that way. She confided to Céline that she regarded the trials of this period of her life as a very special plan of God for helping her grow in holiness. And Pope Benedict XV suggests that same possibility about Thérèse in the years after her mother's death:

Might it not have been the will of Almighty God to effect in her this sudden transformation, this early determination, to adorn her soul with the qualities of spiritual childhood . . . ?

In the testimony at the trial we discover a frequent use of the phrase, "She was an angel." She was called "an angel" by Père Pichon, Abbé Ducellier, Mlle. Philippe (an old lady who was sacristan at St. Pierre's), and of course by her sisters. The use of the phrase by these witnesses, and the many others who employed it, can be accepted in the common usage as it is applied to quiet and obedient little children, and in that sense it is merely a complimentary and somewhat affected remark. Or it could be used in a more literal sense, as apparently Pope Pius XI employed it when he said that she was of a nature "more angelic than human." That would seem to be the intent of the witnesses in Thérèse's case; she was an astonishingly holy child, almost too good for this earth. The old sacristan, Mlle. Philippe, had frequent opportunity to observe Thérèse around the streets of Lisieux, and especially in the Church of St. Pierre when the child came for Mass each morning and for a visit to the Blessed Sacrament later in the day. Speaking to her helper in the sacristy one day, she said:

That little Thérèse Martin is a real angel. I will be really surprised if she lives a long time; but if she lives, you will see that people will be speaking about her one day, because she will become a saint.

The same kind of testimony was given by Jeanne Guérin, who stated that her parents had great admiration for Thérèse's piety, and she often overheard them say: "This child will not live long, she is too angelic." (In a marginal note next to this testimony, the compilers of the ecclesiastical *Processus* had printed in Latin: "They foresaw the short life of one whose virtues were like those of an angel.")

Pauline also adds to our understanding of this aspect of Thérèse's life, stating: "From her infancy she had a presentiment that her life would be short."

Physically, Thérèse was an attractive girl. The witnesses are in agreement about that, adding that she seemed rather indifferent to her prettiness. None of them, for example, can remember her ever studying herself in a mirror. Thérèse wrote in the autobiography that her first awareness of the fact she was pretty came on the beach at Trouville where the Martins were vacationing with the Guérin family at their summer house. She was walking on the sand, hand in hand with her father, when they met a couple and became engaged in conversation with them. Was the young girl his daughter? the lady and gentleman asked M. Martin. What a pretty little girl, they said; but M. Martin made a quick gesture for them to cease flattering his daughter. "I saw that he signaled them not to pay me compliments," she wrote. "It was the first time I had heard myself called pretty, and I was pleased because I did not believe I was."

She was tall for her age, graceful and reserved. Her blond hair was worn long and curled at the end in tiny ringlets. The testimony at the trial reveals that she presented a pleasant and compelling image to the people who knew her—the composed little blond girl with the gentle smile and the sad eyes, walking through the streets of Lisieux with her father, playing games with her sister and cousin, kneeling upright in church, her hands clasped, her eyes gazing tenderly at the tabernacle.

Victoire, the family maid who was the central figure in some of the childhood episodes Thérèse mentions in the autobiography, did not testify at the trial, but one day after Thérèse's death she appeared at the parlor of the Carmelite convent and recalled her former mistress:

Truly Mlle. Thérèse was not ordinary. I loved all of you, but Mlle. Thérèse had something that none of you others had. She was like an angel. *Ça m'a frappée!*

CHAPTER III

GROWTH AND ILLUMINATION

1. THE ILLNESS

The year following Thérèse's enrollment at school, Pauline entered the Carmelite convent in Lisieux, and for the second time Thérèse found herself suddenly bereft of a "mother." It was another painful blow for the young girl, afflicting her sharply, and some five months later she was taken to bed with that strange illness which saw her haunted with hallucinations and tossed about with convulsions. She was suddenly cured, as she herself describes it in the autobiography, through the intervention of the Blessed Virgin.

Thérèse recounts some of the clinical facts about her illness in the autobiography, and more details were supplied by the witnesses at the trial, but withal the episode does not lend itself to an easy diagnosis or solution.

The dates and events can be recorded easily, and the inception point is probably Pauline's entrance into the convent in October of 1882. The departure of her older sister and her *petite mère* was a shattering blow to Thérèse: she had just been reassembling her world after the loss of her mother five years previously when she was forced to see it fall apart again. Thérèse had not been privy to Pauline's plans, and only learned of them when she overheard a conversation shortly before Pauline's entrance. On the morning of October 2, the whole family attended Mass together, then Pauline stepped through the cloister doors as they were bolted behind her. "I believe that if the whole world crumbled around me," Thérèse wrote, "I would not have noticed it; I looked at the blue sky and wondered how the sun could shine so brightly when my own soul was plunged in sadness."

She was allowed to visit her sister every Thursday with her family, but the actual time she obtained to talk with Pauline was only a few minutes and her sense of loss was not assuaged. "It is astonishing to observe how my spirit unfolded in the midst of that suffering; unfolded to such an extent that I soon fell ill." Near the end of that year she began to suffer constant headaches, and in the following March a serious attack occurred. M. Martin had taken Marie and Léonie to Paris for a few days, while Thérèse and Céline remained at Lisieux with the Guérins. One evening M. Guérin began to reminisce about Thérèse's mother, and as the ten-year-old girl listened the old wound was reopened and tears began to course down her face. The astonished uncle said that she was too sensitive (Thérèse: *"Il dit que j'avis trop de coeur"*) and he tried to distract her by making plans for interesting things to do during the Easter vacation from school. But that evening as she was disrobing she suffered an attack of shivering which resembled a cold chill, and was put to bed with hot water bottles. But the trembling continued throughout the night, and the physician, Dr. Notta, was summoned in the morning; he was perplexed and his first hesitant diagnosis was St. Vitus's dance (or chorea). Thérèse could not be moved home, even when a distressed M. Martin rushed back to see his ailing daugh-

ter. The illness endured for a little over a week, and Thérèse records that her distraught father thought she would
either die or go mad. However, the date of Pauline's investiture ceremony at the Carmel was rapidly approaching, a day which the family had planned on for a long
time, and Thérèse's illness strangely subsided, allowing
her to attend the ceremony with no difficulty at all. She
returned with her family to Les Buissonnets, was put to
bed again, and the next morning the full crisis of her illness started.

From April seventh to May thirteenth Thérèse was confined to bed, and during that time she suffered a strange
mélange of hallucinations, comas, and convulsions. She
appeared to be in delirium, crying out against unseen and
terrifying objects. Marie said that she was tossed violently about in bed, hitting her head on the bedboards,
as if some strange force were assailing her. Céline observed that these convulsions would sometimes resemble
the actions of a gymnastic. Once some nails on the wall
took on the appearance for her of large black fingers and
she cried out: "I'm afraid, I'm afraid!" On another occasion her father stood sadly by her bed, his hat in his
hands, and Thérèse's eyes fixed on the hat while she
cried: "Oh, the black beast!" Léonie remembers that Thérèse would occasionally be thrown out of bed, and one
Sunday when the rest of the family was attending high
Mass, Léonie remained behind to watch her sister and
was witness to one particularly frightening incident: since
her sister seemed to be resting quietly, she left the room
for a few minutes, but when she returned Thérèse had
thrown herself on the tile floor and was wedged, head
down, between the bed and the wall. But amazingly,
Léonie recalled, her sister was unhurt.

The convulsive movements of her body were the most
strange phenomena of all. The witnesses talk of "rotary

movements of the whole body of which she was completely incapable in good health." Marie speaks about
one gymnastic on which all the sisters pass comment:

> . . . she rose up on her knees, and without using her
> hands, laid her head on the bed and brought her knees
> up over her head. And in this position, in which she
> certainly should have become exposed, she always re-
> mained modestly clothed; and it was so astonishing
> that I can only explain it by attributing it to some heav-
> enly intervention.

M. Martin sent some money for Masses to the Church
of Our Lady of Victories in Paris, and the whole family
began to implore the Blessed Virgin to help Thérèse. A
novena of Masses had been requested and while it was in
progress Thérèse suffered her worst and final attack.
Marie described it at the trial and she supplied many
more details than those recounted in the autobiography.
The most upsetting incident of the attack for this closely-
knit family occurred when Thérèse turned away from a
drink offered by her sister, crying: "They want to kill me,
they want to poison me." Stricken, Marie turned toward
a statue of the Blessed Virgin in the bedroom and began
to pray for her sister while Céline and Léonie joined her
on their knees. Thérèse writes:

> Since there was no help on the earth, the poor little
> Thérèse also turned towards the Mother of Heaven
> and prayed with all her heart that she might have pity
> on her. All at once, the Blessed Virgin appeared to me
> in her beauty, more beautiful than anything I have
> ever seen before, and her face had an expression of
> indescribable kindness and tenderness. But what pen-
> etrated to the depth of my soul was the "entrancing

smile of the Blessed Virgin." With that, my illness just disappeared, and two large tears formed in my eyes and coursed softly down my cheeks; but they were tears of an unmitigated joy.

This marked the termination of Thérèse's illness, and except for two occasions in the month following when she fainted and remained in a state of rigidity for a few minutes, there was never any recurrence. She rose from bed, the next day she was out visiting the Guérins, she returned to school, and life resumed its normal pattern for her.

Dr. Notta, who treated her throughout the course of her illness, was an eminent and highly respected physician in Lisieux, and he represented some of the finest medical skill available at that time in Normandy; he was, however, frankly confused by the whole affair. There was a variety of conflicting and unidentifiable symptoms which he eventually diagnosed as St. Vitus's dance, but Jeanne Guérin testified that he was uncertain about it and felt it could very well be something else. Mystified by the illness and unsatisfied with his diagnosis, he treated Thérèse by ordering daily massages and sponge baths and the application of wet compresses, all of which seemed to have no effect. Dr. Notta did, though, make one negative diagnosis: "You may call it whatever you want, but as far as I am concerned it is not hysteria."

Thérèse, on her part, regarded the illness as the direct work of the devil. "The illness which I suffered," she wrote to Pauline, "certainly was caused by the devil, who was enraged at your entry into Carmel and at all the injury our family was going to do to him in the future." And elsewhere in the autobiography she wrote: "I believe that the devil obtained some exterior power over me but was not able to reach my soul or my spirit." Thérèse's sisters and the rest of the family readily adopted this view and testified to it during the trial, but a number of modern commentators, Robo and Goerres among them, regard this view as curiously naïve, something prompted by pious minds who knew nothing of modern psychiatry and could only explain the unusual by ascribing it to the devil.

A clarification, if not a diagnosis, of Thérèse's illness preoccupied the ecclesiastical officials who worked on her cause. In the *Super Dubio* decree of the Congregation of Rites in 1921, only one specific objection to Thérèse's canonization is cited: her childhood illness. The decree reads:

> One of these (objections) seems worthy of mention since, had it been sustained, it would have substantially affected the entire Cause. It concerns the illness of Sister Thérèse, which exercised so malignant a power upon herself and her actions as to cast suspicion on her sanctity, and to disturb seriously that which is the natural foundation of all heroic virtue.

This same problem has disturbed Thérèse's commentators through the years, and a number of different diagnoses have been offered. Dr. Notta's hesitant diagnosis does not find much favor today, since there are too many nonconformable symptoms for St. Vitus's dance. For one thing, Thérèse gained periods of respite in her illness during which, as she recounts in the autobiography, she was able to do such careful work as weaving crowns of flowers and cutting cardboard figures—something which the average patient with St. Vitus's dance (or chorea) is unable to do. Nor does the epilepsy theory prove very attractive either, since Thérèse was painfully conscious of what she was doing during the attacks, and retained a complete recollection of everything after the attack.

The theory of simple hysteria is not a satisfactory one today, and one of the many reasons is that Thérèse had a number of her attacks when she was unwatched. Modern psychiatry informs us that a true hysteric needs some kind of an audience before he has a seizure.

Thomas Verner Moore offers an engaging theory in his *Heroic Sanctity and Insanity*.[1] He suspects that Thérèse's illness was pyelonephritis, an infection of the kidney which can cause a toxic delirium. Dom Moore, a priest-psychiatrist, notes Thérèse's symptoms—the persistent headaches, the chills, the prostration, the delirium—and concludes that they concur accurately with a clinical picture of pyelonephritis. This disease can produce many of the aspects of Thérèse's illness, even the hallucinations and convulsions. A competent pediatrician today would certainly consider the possibility of pyelonephritis in a ten-year-old child with Thérèse's symptoms, but that was not the case in 1883. Dom Moore's thesis is intriguing, and it is original, too, since he is the first author to raise the possibility of this diagnosis.

The nervous breakdown theory has been popularized and sensationalized greatly in the last two decades, and there are enough inexplicable facts in the episode to allow room for theorizing. (But might we note an interesting reversal of modern times: while in former centuries the inexplicable was immediately ascribed to the devil, today the inexplicable—or even that which is not readily conformable—is immediately ascribed to mental aberration.) Some of the facts seem to indicate undeniably that, as Robo states, Thérèse "was heading for a nervous breakdown" (p. 67). There was the despondency over her mother's death, her unhappiness at school, and the new

crisis of Pauline's departure for the convent; and when
M. Guérin plunged her into a session of reminiscences
about happier days, something snapped and Thérèse lost
control as she was assailed by hallucinations and violent
contortions. We seem to be observing a pattern, an uncomfortable pattern in which an emotional shock culminates in a mental ailment.

But there are a number of facts which do not fit the
pattern or conform to the syndrome of mental failure as
we understand it. The most interesting of these is Thérèse's astonishing statement that, despite the violence of
her illness, she never lost the use of reason. She wrote:

> . . . my words and actions did not at all correspond
> to my thoughts; I seemed to be almost in constant delir-
> ium, saying senseless words, and yet I am sure that I
> was not deprived of the use of my reason for a single
> moment.

Thérèse underlines that last phrase in the autobiography because it stands in apparent contradiction to
everything else we have observed in her illness. Yet,
Marie testified to the same phenomenon at the trial:

> I am certain that even in the severest crises of her ill-
> ness, the Servant of God retained the use of her higher
> faculties; she was subjected to upheavals in her senses,
> but she was always perfectly aware of it. My own ob-
> servation convinced me, and she herself assured me of
> it later on, that during the attacks she heard and under-
> stood everything being said around her; and during
> that final attack, which lasted for about an hour, she
> prayed interiorly to the Blessed Virgin during every
> moment of it.

Thérèse, therefore, was suffering hallucinations and uttering strange nonsenses, yet throughout it all she remained in perfect interior possession of herself, aware of it, distressed by it, and praying for deliverance. This fact alone might make us wonder if we are dealing with sheer mental illness, and it might make us re-examine Thérèse's assertion that her illness was the result of some demonic influence.

Frau Goerres writes: "As we have seen, Thérèse herself also states that her illness was produced by the envy of the devil; but we must remember that her opinion was formed when she was eleven and a half years old and simply took over her sisters' views" (p. 417). This is not exactly correct, for Thérèse first put the blame on herself as she wrote in the autobiography: ". . . I am convinced now that it was the work of the devil, but for a long time after my cure I believed I had made myself ill on purpose and that was a true martyrdom for me." In actuality, it was only after she entered the convent a number of years later that she finally decided the illness had been effected by demonic influence; and it was twelve years after the ordeal that she wrote her evaluation of it in her memoirs. Thus, Thérèse's diagnosis as she presents it in the autobiography is not the uneducated reaction of a ten-year-old girl; rather it is the considered opinion of a person who had weathered the trials of the spiritual life and who had gained the supernatural prudence and insight possessed by souls in the higher stages of spiritual union. Such an opinion cannot lightly be dismissed.

Thérèse stated that the devil was enraged at all the harm the Martin family was going to do to him, and Goerres calls this "a curiously naïve reason" (p. 77). But is it? Hagiography is replete with episodes in which the devil takes physical vengeance for work done contrary to his interests. Witness a famous case which occurred in

France only twenty-five years before Thérèse's illness: the Curé of Ars, St. John Marie Vianney, had to suffer the physical violence of *le grappin*, the devil, who attacked him in the evenings, tossing him about and throwing furniture. And the Curé had to endure this for thirty-five years. There is at least one marked similarity between the cases of Thérèse and the Curè: they both were thrown and catapulted by some strange force, and they both, inexplicably, remained uninjured. Would it be groundless to assert that just as the devil was enraged at the Curé of Ars, he might well be angered at the Martin family, and at the youngest daughter in particular?

Furthermore, Thérèse's somersaults were strangely mysterious. According to Marie's testimony, which we cited above, she appeared to lose control of herself and began turning somersaults on the bed; but as she drew her legs up over her head, her nightgown continued to cover her completely so that she was not subjected to any embarrassing exposure. The Martin sisters all regarded this as humanly impossible (*dans cette attitude qui devait infalliblement la découvrir*, Marie said), and they considered it the result of some heavenly influence. And yet hagiographical accounts of diabolical obsession note the same phenomenon: God will permit the devil to harrass an individual, but never to cause any loss of modesty.

We have, therefore, an interesting array of clinical details: Thérèse's own mature assertion that her illness was caused by demonic powers; her complete possession of her interior faculties during the most violent attacks; her immunity from physical harm, despite the fact that she was thrown against the headboards, and dove head first to the tile floor; her preservation of modesty during the gyrations. No amount of rationalization or medical diagnosis can argue those facts away; they remain, collectively, inexplicable in terms of our human sciences. Are we witnessing another case of diabolic obsession? The Papal documents give no definitive answer, but Pope Pius XI in the decree for the beatification seems to lean toward that opinion:

> She was afflicted with a serious illness whose nature and cure were mysterious; and it was the considered opinion of her family that her sickness was caused by the devil who foresaw the harm she would do him; and that opinion is confirmed by her amazing and sudden cure after special prayers to the Blessed Virgin.

According to Catholic theology, the devil is a fallen angel endowed with extraordinary intelligence; he is allowed, in God's plan, to work for his own evil purposes, most often in a secret and unobtrusive manner, but sometimes in an open and abusive way, as in the case of the Curé of Ars. The question before us now is not why God allows the devil to operate—if that question can ever be answered adequately in this life—but whether or not Thérèse Martin was the object of diabolical obsession. Father Marie-Eugene, O.C.D., the eminent spiritual theologian, believes she was;[2] and this is also the contention of the Spanish scholar, Padre Alberto Moneo, in his *La Espiritualidad de Santa Teresa de Lisieux*.[3] Their conclusions are based on a careful investigation of all the details of Thérèse's illness, and if their evaluations serve no other purpose they at least present a theory which takes into account, coordinates, and explains *every* aspect of the illness.

Père François de Sainte-Marie, O.C.D., the editor of the *Manuscrits Autobiographiques*, has undoubtedly done more direct and immediate research on St. Thérèse than anyone else living in the world today; he produced the original version of her manuscript, he examined all the

documents, and he was given free access to the archives
of the Carmel in Lisieux. He deserves, at the very least, a
hearing in the present discussion. Commenting on Thérèse's statement that the devil had been given some external power over her, he states, calmly: "A number of
unusual occurrences during the illness would seem to
authorize that opinion."[4] And Père François' comment
would seem to summarize the problem.

Five years after her cure, during her pilgrimage trip,
Thérèse visited the Church of Our Lady of Victories in
Paris, and as she knelt before the shrine a gentle sense of
confirmation settled over her, bestowing an assurance that
the Blessed Virgin had truly appeared to her. She wrote:

> I am unable to describe what I felt kneeling at her feet
> . . . The Blessed Virgin made me believe that it was
> truly she who smiled at me and cured me.

She carried this conviction throughout her life. When
she was moved into the convent infirmary some two and
a half months before her death, she discovered the statue
from Les Buissonnets which had, in the intervening years,
been donated to the Carmel. She gazed at it wistfully,
and Marie remembers her comment: "It is not like that
first time . . . That other time, you know very well that it
was not just a statue."

Father Robo, on the other hand, contends that Thérèse did not enjoy a vision of the Blessed Virgin; he believes that it was all part of the nervous breakdown. "The
religious mind of the child created the heavenly picture
which alone could bring her comfort and recovery," he
says (p. 69). In response to this opinion, we might state
first that the Bull of Canonization claims: "She was gen-

erously freed from that serious and mystifying illness, which she suffered when she was ten, through the help of the Blessed Virgin, who appeared to her, smiling." Secondly, Thérèse herself firmly believed she had received a vision, and in her last poem wrote:

> Oh, you who came to smile on me at the dawn of life,
> Come once again to smile on me . . . for, Mother, the
>   night is near.

Thérèse's two relapses do not necessarily make the genuineness of the cure suspect, as has been suggested by some commentators. For one thing, there is no comparison between her long illness and the two momentary failures she suffered: Léonie says that Thérèse only fell into a dead faint for a few minutes during which her body became rigid, and then it was all over. And even if these two incidents were considered part of her major illness, they would not contradict a miraculous cure, since many cures we accept as miraculous are accomplished in stages spanning a number of weeks or months; witness some of the cures at Lourdes. And the only aftereffects of her illness— if they were aftereffects—occurred during the month following her cure.

2. ADOLESCENCE

The years from 1883 to 1886 were years of growth and development for Thérèse. The outstanding event of this period, from her own viewpoint, was her first Communion on May 8, 1884; it was, she wrote, "the most beautiful day of my life." The eleven-year-old child experienced, on that day, a new closeness to Christ, a new sense of being loved by Him. In the autobiography, she is reluctant to reveal all the details of that experience, and it is the one place where she exhibits any reluctance at all to disclose her most intimate thoughts. She writes:

> Ah, how sweet was that first kiss Jesus gave to my soul. It was a kiss of love, and I knew that I was loved. I said to Him: "I love you and I give myself to you forever."

She cried after the reception of her first Communion, but her tears were, as she wrote, tears of joy. A month later, she received for the second time and with equally profound sentiments. From that time she tried to receive as frequently as she was allowed by her confessor; the custom of the time discouraged frequent Communion, yet she received permission to receive on a number of feast days, some twenty-two times a year. Concomitant with this, she conceived an intense desire to detach herself from material things and to suffer for God. "Until then," she wrote, "I suffered without loving suffering, but from this time on I was conscious of a real love for it." She was fond of reciting the phrase from the *Imitation*, "Oh, Jesus, unspeakable sweetness, change into bitterness for me all the consolations of this life," and she said it with full understanding of all its implications.

Her religious perceptions were becoming even more precise, more mature. A careful reading of her autobiography—a reading that can prescind from the stilted expressions of the late Romantic period—shows that she was rooting herself in a spirituality of the most mature and valid kind. "I experienced the desire," she wrote, "of loving only God and of finding my joy only in Him." This statement, which bears such a strong resemblance to the phrases used by St. John of the Cross, demonstrates how far removed she was, even at that early date, from the sentimental piety some people have associated with her.

Her prayer seems to have been answered, and during a retreat at the abbey in May of 1885 she fell prey to an attack of scruples which lasted for almost a year and a half. Scruples, a not infrequent malady of the spiritual life, consist in an anxiety and overconscientiousness about moral issues and make the agonized soul fear sin unreasonably. "It is impossible for me to describe what I suffered during that year and a half," she wrote. "My most simple thoughts and actions became a source of trouble for me; and the only way I could get relief was by telling Marie about them." Marie prudently dismissed her sister's scruples, advising her not even to bother mentioning them in confession. Thérèse followed Marie's splendid advice with such exactitude that "my confessor had no idea of my pitiable condition," and "I could have passed for the least scrupulous person on the earth."

Her deliverance from scruples came shortly after Marie's departure for the convent. Lacking a confidante to whom she could tell her problems, Thérèse turned to the four Martin children who had died in infancy and prayed for help. "An answer was not long in coming; very soon a delightful sense of peace flooded my soul, and I realized that I was loved in heaven as well as on earth." This marked the end of her siege of scruples.

Two things might be noted about her scruples. First, her sudden cure does not, of itself, indicate any extraordinary intervention from heaven, since in the spiritual life scruples are frequently a temporary situation which disappear as suddenly as they arose. Secondly, Thérèse had enough self-mastery to refrain from mentioning her scruples in confession, which indicates that her problems were not as serious or debilitating as they are in many cases.

Any confessor or director with experience in this area can testify that the scrupulous person is almost driven by a compulsion to confess these worries and doubts and cannot be dissuaded from doing so; the fact that Thérèse never even mentioned them once—an unbelievable thing for a truly scrupulous person—would seem to suggest that her scruples were of a minor and controllable variety, despite the anguish they caused to the sensitive thirteen-year-old girl.

Père François places the immediate cause of Thérèse's scruples in the retreat she attended in May of 1885 at the abbey.[5] The notes she made during the retreat lectures are still extant, and they recount sober and serious warnings about mortal sin, death, judgment, and the necessity of making a good confession. Thérèse's notes indicate that the lectures were much too grim for a group of adolescent girls, and it is not inconceivable that they could have precipitated an attack of scruples.

Those who hold the nervous breakdown thesis see her scruples as one more manifestation of her mental condition. But there is another group of reputable and eminent theologians (Father Garrigou-LaGrange, O.P.; Father Marie-Eugene, O.C.D.; and Father Gabriel of St. Mary Magdalen, O.C.D.) who maintain that her scruples were the result of God's purifying action in her soul;[6] this theory is based on the doctrine of St. John of the Cross that God sometimes sends scruples as part of His program of bringing an individual to a greater holiness.

In the early spring of 1886, M. Martin withdrew Thérèse from the abbey school and placed her under the instruction of a tutor, Mme. Papinau. The decision at that particular time was occasioned by the fact that Céline

had finished at the abbey some months before, and Thérèse, who had never liked the convent, now found herself
without even her sister's companionship. Furthermore,
she had been suffering from headaches and had a fatigued appearance, and the family felt the new arrangement would be more satisfactory, which, in fact, it proved
to be. She took lessons with the old tutor for at least a year
and a half—perhaps a little longer—and then she discontinued formal study when she was about fifteen. Thérèse,
therefore, had about as much schooling as the average
girl in Normandy at that time: Marie, for example, finished school at fifteen, and Céline at sixteen.

At the trial, her sisters related an interesting fact: M.
Guérin, their uncle, was under the impression at this time
that Thérèse was a slow, below-average student. We know
from her own testimony, and from that of Abbé Domin
and the teachers at the abbey, that she was a superior
student. The only explanation for M. Guérin's failure to
recognize his niece's brilliance is that Thérèse was careful never to reveal it. This is more amazing when we consider the close relationship between the two families and
the fact that Thérèse spent every Thursday at the Guérins'
household. We know, from the story she recounts in the
autobiography, that there was at least one occasion when
she desperately wanted to manifest her intelligence before
the class; yet she had enough self-mastery at the Guérins'
to deny herself this satisfaction. It is another appealing insight into the control the young girl possessed.

A similar illustration is offered by Marie. M. Martin
had arranged for Céline to take art lessons (she was the
most artistically talented of the five sisters, at least by the
norms of late Romantic art), and he subsequently asked
Thérèse if she would like lessons too. Marie overheard the
offer and protested that Thérèse had no talent and it

would be a waste of money. Thérèse remained silent, and her father dropped the matter. Years later in the convent, Thérèse admitted that she very much wanted to take the lessons. "But you should have said something about it," Marie told her. "Yes, but I did not want to refuse anything to the good God," Thérèse answered.

Despite these indications of her firmness of character and self-descipline, she confesses she still had faults during this period. She records an incident which took place while they were vacationing one summer with the Guérins at Trouville. Marie Guérin, her cousin, had been suffering from continual headaches, and she made the most of her infirmity: crying, eliciting sympathy. Thérèse said that she suffered constant headaches, too, but never cried over them; one evening, however, she decided she wanted similar compassion and forced some tears. The family quickly gathered around her, asked her the trouble, and when she told them she had a headache, they failed to show her any particular sympathy. "I understood then the fable of the donkey and the little dog: I was just like the donkey who saw how the dog was petted and, therefore, put his heavy hoof on the table to receive some of the kisses. *Mais hélas!* Although I was not beaten like the donkey, I learned a lesson which cured me for the rest of my life of trying to attract attention."

Thérèse's most vexing fault still endured: her sensitivity, that annoying habit of being so easily hurt. She writes that if she inadvertently offended someone, she would begin to cry, and then after she had calmed herself, she would cry about having cried. "Reasoning about it did no good, and I was not able to correct myself of that wicked fault." But on Christmas of 1887, just before her fifteenth birthday, a strange and instant alchemy produced in her a transformation which all efforts had been unable to accomplish. She called it her "conversion."

3. CONVERSION

Thérèse had just returned from midnight Mass with her father and Céline, and she was mounting the stairs to remove her coat when she overheard her father speaking downstairs. M. Martin was looking at some shoes arranged before the fireplace, shoes which had been gaily stuffed with presents and candy for Thérèse, and he was waiting for her to reappear and inspect her gifts. "Well, I am glad this is the last year we have to do this," he said wearily. Thérèse had just reached the turn in the landing between the first and second floors and was out of her father's view, but his words had drifted up. Céline, standing beside her, knew how deeply the careless remark would afflict her sister, and advised her to wait and compose herself before descending to open the gifts. "But Thérèse was different now, Jesus had changed her heart! Pushing back my tears I went downstairs at once, and with heart beating rapidly I took out my gifts and laid them before Papa." Thérèse also noted that Céline thought she must be dreaming as she watched her in astonishment merrily playing before her father: this was the Thérèse who ordinarily would be dissolved in tears, deeply offended by her father's comment, but here she was, spirited, charming, smiling. This was no momentary conquest, however, but a radical and lasting change. "On that glorious night the third period of my life began, the most beautiful of all, the one most filled with graces." Céline spoke of it at the trial:

I was a witness to that sudden change and I thought I was in a dream when, for the first time, I saw her conquer something which would ordinarily have left her desolate. Instead she began to make my father happy. This change was decisive and never again was she dominated by any sensitivity. That transformation was not limited only to a new self-possession but, at the same time, her soul could be seen to develop and grow in the practice of zeal and charity. She dreamed about the salvation of souls and busied herself, enthusiastically and generously, with the conversion of sinners. In a short time, God had drawn Thérèse out of the tight circle in which she lived. Freed from her scruples and her excessive sensitiveness, her spirit expanded. She was captivated by a pressing desire to learn new things, a desire which was directed by her total dedication to God. Spiritual books were her daily nourishment, and she knew the *Imitation* by heart. Holy Communion and daily assistance at Mass became her delights. Jesus was the director of her soul. Since both Marie and Pauline were already in Carmel, Thérèse and I drew closer and closer to each other. Each evening at the windows of the belvedere, we exchanged thoughts about eternity. Those words of St. John of the Cross, "to suffer and be despised," were often on our lips and inflamed our hearts. Being despised seemed to us the only thing desirable on this earth, and suffering the only good worth envying.

Those commentators who reduce Thérèse's life to a study in psychological abnormality have always had some trouble fitting the experience of Christmas, 1887, into their thesis; it is inexplicable in terms of human psychology, and those commentators usually pass over it quickly, perhaps dismissing it as the beginning point of a new maturation. But it is not something that can be easily dismissed. Her change was, as Céline said at the trial, "abrupt and without transition," and people simply do not mature and change in that manner: there is ordinarily a period of improvement, a program of gradual development sprinkled with failures and falls and new resolutions until finally a new plateau is reached. Thérèse achieved that plateau instantly and was projected into a new stage of spiritual living. Some years later, she wrote about that Christmas night in a letter to Abbé Belliere: ". . . Jesus, who became a child for love of me, deigned to bring me forth from the swaddling clothes and imperfections of infancy. He transformed me so utterly that I no longer recognized myself."

Thérèse's sudden maturation and her immediate involvement in a new phase of spiritual living would seem to indicate the infusion of some special grace from God. Father Marie-Eugene, O.C.D., explains it, in the terminology of spiritual theology, as a "substantial touching," a clumsy term which he further defines as an operation of the Holy Spirit infusing wisdom and bestowing new vigor to the personality.[7] In this explanation, Thérèse's transformation is not strictly miraculous, but rather the result of the Holy Spirit's activity ordinarily bestowed on souls making genuine and marked progress in the spiritual life; this is a phenomenon frequently discussed by spiritual theologians, and often observed in the lives of the saints. One of the most graphic and careful accounts of this phenomenon is given by St. Teresa in Chapter XXVII of her *Life* as she describes her own experiences with it and teaches her readers how to recognize it in their lives.[8] She writes: ". . . a single one of these favors suffices to change [the soul] altogether and make it love nothing save Him who, without any labor on its part, renders it capable of receiving such great blessings . . ."

If hagiography and spiritual theology admit this phenomenon in the lives of other saints, would it not be possible to suggest that it occurred in the life of the young girl who was already so astonishingly holy, who had for eleven years been "refusing nothing to the good God"?

4. VOCATION

One of the most notable effects of Thérèse's "conversion" was her new and deep preoccupation with the apostolate. One Sunday at church, a holy card slipped from her prayer book, revealing a picture of Christ's pierced hand, and she suddenly experienced an overwhelming desire to become involved in the conversion of sinners. ". . . I was distressed that the blood of Christ fell to the earth without anyone carefully gathering it up, and I resolved to stand in spirit at the foot of the Cross to gather up this Divine Dew and apply it to souls. That cry of Jesus on the Cross, 'I thirst,' echoed continually in my heart."

The plight of one Pranzini, an Alexandrian convicted of murdering three women in the notorious "case of the *Rue Montaigne*," came to her attention and she resolved to pray for the condemned man who refused to make his peace with God. She began a program of resolute prayer for him, had Masses offered, and even enlisted Céline's help when her sister forced the secret from her. In this, her first case, she asked God for some sign of success:

Deep in my heart I felt certain our request would be granted, but to encourage me in continuing to pray for sinners, I told God that even though I was sure He would pardon poor Pranzini and that I would believe it even if he did not go to confession or give any sign of repentance (this was the kind of confidence I had in the infinite mercy of Jesus), I would still like to see just one sign of repentance for my own consolation.

She received her sign in the morning edition of *La Croix* which related the story of Pranzini's execution and final act of repentance when he grasped a crucifix on the gallows, kissing it three times in a gesture of contrition.

She continued to pray for Pranzini's soul throughout her life, and years later in the convent when her family wanted to give her a present, she asked that money be donated to be applied to Masses for him; "He is my child," she said, "and I must not forget him now."

Marceline Husé remembers Thérèse at this period teaching catechism to some of the poor children of Lisieux and giving them presents. She observed Thérèse denying herself candy and cake served at home, carefully secreting it away, and later giving it to the children. These children seemed to be genuinely fond of Thérèse, and Marceline has preserved a recollection of them clustered around her, climbing up on her knee, and listening attentively while she told them stories and taught them catechism lessons. Yet her new absorption in the apostolate had nothing of the fanatic about it; she was no uncompromising zealot. Marceline recalls one occasion on a walk when they passed a workman who was cursing and swearing eloquently: Thérèse immediately turned to her companion and said they should not judge him harshly because he had probably received less grace than they and was to be considered more unfortunate than culpable. (An eminently sane and charitable attitude, so unlike that of many people who become convinced they have a mission in life.)

In the summer of 1887, Thérèse spent some weeks at Trouville with the Guérin family, and when she returned to Lisieux she kept up a lively correspondence with Marie and Jeanne, who were staying at the beach for the rest of the summer. Some of Thérèse's letters to her cousins are still extant, and they constitute an amazing correspondence in the light of what her autobiography tells us she was experiencing that summer. Her letters are the typical chatty, effusive, somewhat trivial letters of a teen-age girl: she inquires about her cousin's toothache, describes two bluebirds she had purchased for Céline, encourages Marie to take walks in the park, and laments that eight silkworms she was keeping had died. During the period these letters were written, her apostolic instincts were coming vitally alive: the episode with the picture of Christ's pierced hand took place, as well as her program of prayer for Pranzini. Yet none of this appears in her letters—only toothaches and bluebirds and silkworms. These letters, placed alongside her autobiography, present proof of the complete integration of her life, of her normalcy, and one more example of Pope Pius XI's phrase, ". . . without going beyond the common order of things."

When Thérèse was two years old she made the statement, "I will become a religious," but she admits she said it with no real understanding of what it meant. As the years passed, however, she became aware of the full significance of the religious life and was able to make a valid decision to become a nun. Pauline and Marie were already in the Carmel of Lisieux, and she decided to enter the same convent. The ecclesiastical judges at the trial asked whether she entered that particular convent merely to join her sisters, but it was roundly denied by all the witnesses. Léonie registered an emphatic *no*, claiming that her sister's only consideration was the love of God, and she recounted Thérèse's statement in the autobiography where she said if she could not enter Carmel, she would go to a refuge with repentant girls. Pauline testified that she asked her little sister one day if she wanted to enter the Carmel because of her sisters, and Thérèse appeared stunned by the question. "No," she answered, "it is because of the good God alone." Therefore, she was not seeking a continuation of life at Les Buissonnets, a fact vividly demonstrated by her attitude toward

her sisters in the convent and by her later decision to volunteer for the Carmel in Viet-Nam.

A Carmelite convent is an institute of contemplatives
dedicated to prayer, penance, and union with God; there
is no external work, no teaching, no labor in a hospital,
no catechizing, only the monastic regime with its hours
of prayer, its daily sacrifices, its continual subjection to
religious authority. Yet St. Teresa of Avila's intention in
founding the reformed Carmel was an apostolic one: she
wanted her nuns to win souls and help the Church by
their hidden lives of prayer and penance. Thérèse Martin
was a ready inheritor of this doctrine: acting under the
impulse of the apostolic thrust she had received in her
"conversion," she decided that she could win more souls
as a Carmelite nun than in any other religious order.
Céline stated that her sister considered the religious life
primarily as a means of saving souls and that Thérèse
had first wanted to be a foreign missionary but eventually
concluded she could do more good in Carmel. Céline remembers that when Thérèse was fourteen she one day
hurriedly laid aside a missionary magazine she was reading, saying she had such an ardent desire for that kind of
life she would want to join the missionary congregation
if she read any more. A few years after her admittance to
the Carmel, she wrote to Céline: "Is not the apostolate of
prayer more elevated than that of the word; our mission,
as Carmelites, is to form apostolic workers who will save
thousands of souls."

And when, during the formal ecclesiastical investigation preceding her religious profession, she was asked
why she had entered Carmel, she stated simply: "I have
come to Carmel to save souls and especially to pray for
priests."

Thérèse was only fourteen when she began to make formal application to the Carmel, hoping she could be ad-

mitted by Christmas of that year. Not everyone, however, shared the nuns' enthusiasm to receive the young girl in the convent. Even her uncle, M. Guérin, thought her too young, and although he finally capitulated, he was very much opposed to it at first. The most formidable opposition was offered by Abbé Delatroette, parish priest of Saint Jacques in Lisieux and superior of the Carmel, who believed she should wait until she was twenty-one.

Some biographers of Thérèse have painted Abbé Delatroette as the implacable foe of the young saint, adamantly determined to thwart her noble aspirations. Admittedly, he was outspoken, irascible, somewhat harsh, and lacking in tact. The witnesses at the trial relate the episode when he entered the cloister on one of the major feasts to visit the ailing Mother Genevieve in the convent infirmary. Mother Gonzague, the prioress, used the opportunity to plead for Thérèse's early admission, in front of the whole community, and the Abbé replied violently: "Again you bring this up. One would think the salvation of the community depended on the entrance of this child. There's nothing to be lost by waiting; let her stay with her father until she's twenty-one. Don't you think I've prayed about this? I ask you not to speak to me about this again." His outburst was so forceful that it brought tears to Mother Gonzague's eyes. And when Thérèse was finally admitted to the convent, the Abbé accompanied her to the cloister door and announced loudly to the nuns: "I hope she will not disappoint your hopes, but let me remind you if it turns out badly the responsibility is yours." But yet, despite these boorish fulminations, it is difficult to see how Abbé Delatroette's basic position could be considered an unjust or imprudent one: Thérèse was only fourteen, and her father, already manifesting the signs of his future illness, was beginning to lean on her more and more; a few years' delay was hardly an unreasonable request. Furthermore, the old priest—he was seventy-one at the time—himself suggested she carry her request to the Bishop and promised, if she obtained his consent, he would do nothing more to oppose it. Finally, Agnes remembers that a few years after Thérèse's entrance, he said of her with tears in his eyes: "Ah, truly, this child is an angel."

While Thérèse was waiting for the Bishop's ultimately favorable reply to her request, M. Martin took her on the pilgrimage to Rome, and a few episodes of that trip afford us some additional insights to her character. Her adventures, on the whole, were those of an enthusiastic tourist: she was amazed and intrigued by the City of Light, the first time she had ever seen it; she found Switzerland indescribably beautiful, and kept running from window to window in the train so as to miss none of it; her readings in history came vividly alive for her when she visited the Palace of the Doges in Venice, the ruins of Pompeii, and the Colosseum in Rome. But her most profound impressions were at religious and pilgrimage sites—Sacre Coeur and Our Lady of Victories in Paris, Assisi, Padua, Loretto, and the churches of Rome.

At Bologna, the train full of French pilgrims was greeted with curiosity and interest since it had been widely reported in the French and Italian press as a tribute of French loyalty to Pope Leo XIII, then the object of a wave of anticlerical animosity in Italy. When Thérèse alighted from the train in Bologna, a group of students from the university was in the station, and one of the students, seeing the tall French girl with the blond hair, threw his arms around her and lifted her off her feet. Céline, who was watching the scene helplessly, saw Thé-

rèse glare at her captor with such fury that he immediately
put her down.

Thérèse's decision to address the Pope directly about
her desire to enter Carmel was not an impulsive act; she
had discussed it at Lisieux before she left and had received encouragement from her sisters. Pauline wrote her
while she was in Italy, again urging her to present her
petition to Leo XIII. But when the Pope seated himself
on his throne to receive the pilgrims, her resolution
began to waver. She writes:

> Before I entered the papal chambers I had made up my
> mind to speak out, but I felt my courage slipping away
> when I saw M. Reverony standing at the Pope's right.
> At the same moment, word was passed along from M.
> Reverony that he did not want us to speak to Leo XIII,
> because the audience had already consumed too much
> time. I turned to consult my dear Céline, and she said:
> "Speak!" A moment later, I was kneeling at the Holy
> Father's feet, kissing his shoe. He gave me his hand,
> but instead of kissing it, I clasped my hands together
> and looked up into his face with tears in my eyes. "Most
> Holy Father, I have a great favor to ask of you," I said.
> He leaned down towards me until his face was almost
> touching mine, and I saw his deep black eyes which
> seemed to penetrate the depths of my soul. "Most Holy
> Father, in honor of your jubilee let me enter Carmel at
> fifteen," I said to him.

Pope Leo XIII glanced at Canon Reverony, who explained the case briefly. Then, softly, the Pope told Thérèse to do what her superior decided, but she insisted
again that everyone would agree if only he gave his consent. "*Allons, allons,*" he said, "you will enter if it be God's
will." She wanted to continue the conversation, but two

Thérèse Martin as a girl of fifteen.

Thérèse at twenty-two.

Thérèse at twenty-three.

The Martin home, *Les Buissonnets,* at Lisieux, where Thérèse lived from the age of four until her entrance into the Carmel of Lisieux.

The Carmel of Lisieux.

ABOVE: St. Thérèse's cell in the Carmel of Lisieux where she wrote the first two sections of her Autobiography.

RIGHT: The cloister garden of the Carmel of Lisieux where St. Thérèse wrote the greater part of the third section of the Autobiography.

BELOW: The infirmary of the Carmel where she wrote the final pages of the Autobiography.

Swiss guards tapped her on the shoulder, and when that did not suffice they lifted her gently by the arms. As she was being raised to her feet, the Pope placed his fingers on her lips and then blessed her; his eyes followed her kindly as she left the chamber.

Some biographers accuse Thérèse of disobedience in speaking to the Pope in the face of the prohibition which had been circulated by Canon Reverony; and others, of obstinacy in pleading her cause (cf. Robo, pp. 84–85). Yet, would any Catholic be truly obliged by a command of a local diocesan official forbidding one to speak with the Father of Christendom; or, to put it in moral perspective, can a local superior prohibit a subject from addressing a higher superior? Pope Leo XIII's successors, at any rate, seem impressed by Thérèse's conduct: Benedict XV called it "a courageous appeal," and Pius XI speaks of how "she overcame her natural timidity." The Popes recognize an aspect of the episode which might very well elude us: the courage Thérèse needed in making her appeal. She was a fourteen-year-old girl from the provinces on her first journey outside Normandy, and her rapid trip to Italy had propelled her into an audience with the Holy Father. We can reasonably assume she was awed, and somewhat bewildered by the pageantry surrounding one of those audiences—the ornate palace, the Swiss guards, the impressive figure of the Pope with his entourage. It entailed no small amount of courage for the young Norman girl to marshal her resources for a direct appeal to the white-frocked figure on the Papal throne.

Thérèse and Céline shared the same hotel room on their journey, and in Rome a complaint was registered against them by one of the priests in the group. The priest, Père Vauquelin, occupied the room next to the two young girls and he complained that they were making too much noise and keeping him awake late at night by their laughter and conversation. Céline remembers that each evening when she and her sister returned from the day's explorations, they would stretch out on the floor, and huddled on the rug, they exchanged their impressions and experiences in Rome. They were too excited to retire, Céline recalled, and were unaware that their animated conversation was keeping awake the priest next door. The complaint was even carried back to Lisieux, and Dom Godfrey Madelaine testified at the trial that Thérèse was said to have been frolicsome (*trop joviale*) in Rome. Dom Madelaine disagreed with the priest's evaluation, though: "But I thought he was too severe in his evaluation of a fifteen-year-old girl who was of a happy and gay character."

Three brief episodes of the trip illuminate another facet of Thérèse. When they were visiting the Colosseum, they found the area open to visitors severely limited. Thérèse was disappointed, for she wanted to walk on the actual ground of the arena. She pondered the situation for a minute, then grabbed Céline by the hand while the two of them scrambled over the ruins and rubble into the arena. Again, at the Church of the Holy Cross in Rome, Thérèse was venerating some relics resting in a hammered gold reliquary when she noticed there was no glass on the reliquary and she could easily put her finger in one of the openings. In this way, she was able to touch what is supposedly one of the nails with which Christ was affixed to the cross. "I was really too bold," she wrote. "Fortunately, the good God who sees into the depths of our hearts knows that my intention was pure and that I would not displease Him for anything in the world; I acted towards Him as a child who does not bother to ask permission but regards her father's treasures as her own." With that statement, she launches into the description of a rather astonishing episode: her violation of a friars' cloister. She discusses a visit to a Discalced Carmelite monastery (Pére François is of the opinion it was Santa Maria della Vittoria in Rome) where the rest of her party was milling around in the public part while she calmly entered the cloistered section reserved for the friars. She immediately encountered an old Carmelite who signaled her frantically to leave, but instead she began pointing to the pictures on the cloister wall and making signs of how she appreciated them. "I suppose he then saw my long hair and my youthful expression and decided I was only a child; he smiled at me kindly and departed, realizing that I was no enemy."

These episodes reveal an adverturesome and slightly uninhibited side of Thérèse Martin, something quite unexpected from the little Norman girl. Her action in entering the friars' cloister is indefensible on purely juridic grounds, but she assures us that subjectively she felt quite justified in doing it and was in perfectly good faith. Her principle was that a monastery was her Father's house, and "I acted towards Him as a child who does not bother to ask permission but regards her father's treasures as her own." We can only judge Thérèse's action, as all people must be judged, on her subjective evaluation of the incident at the time of its occurrence; and she did say, "God . . . knew that my intention was pure and that I would not displease Him for anything in the world." We can very well disagree with the principle she used in entering the cloister, but we cannot fail to be amazed at her freedom of conscience in this episode. Thérèse has been depicted in a number of caricatures as a rather strait-laced, narrow, scrupulous little French girl, but her adventures in Italy simply do not substantiate that evaluation. We see her exhibiting a refreshing nonchalance, and an almost startling freedom and liberty of spirit.

The trip to Italy conferred two special benefits on Thé-rèse. First, it brought her into a closer contact with priests than she had ever known before, and thus she was able to realize that, despite their office, they are still vessels of clay and decidedly in need of our prayers. There is no evidence that she witnessed any untoward episode in this regard; it was simply that her immediate and pro-longed association with a number of priests brought into sharp relief the divine task which has to be performed by these human beings subjected to the vagaries of our na-ture. And from this time, she conceived her life in Car-mel as one of prayer for souls, but especially for priests.

Another advantage the trip conferred was the oppor-tunity to view the larger world outside Normandy and to compare the attractive things she saw with her own as-pirations for a cloistered life. Frau Goerres claims Thé-rèse's attitude toward the world was one of hostility and suspicion, a position of alarm in which the world was re-garded as evil. However, Thérèse's excitement and en-thusiasm during the trip seem to belie that: she enjoyed the world she saw, she was intrigued and fascinated by it; but she was willing to sacrifice it all for a higher good, the love of God. And this is the basis of any valid reli-gious vocation—that the choice is not between good and bad, but between good and better. She manifests these sentiments articulately in the autobiography at the con-clusion of her description of the journey; it is one of the best-written sections of her memoirs, almost sheer poetry, vastly superior to most of the doggerel verse she wrote in the convent.

We stopped at Pisa and Genoa once again, and then on to France. The scenery along the route was magnif-icent; part of the way, the railroad ran along the sea, so close we thought the waves would touch us—it was

evening and there was a storm, all of which made it
more impressive. Then we passed by fields full of orange
trees with the fruit hanging ripe on them, green olive
trees with their delicate leaves, and the graceful palms.
After sunset, we saw all the tiny seaports shining with
thousands of lights, just as the first stars began to glow
in the sky. There was poetry in my heart as I saw these
wonders I was viewing for the first and last time. But
I had no regrets at these things slipping away from me;
my heart was set on greater wonders. I had seen enough
of earth's beauties, now I only wanted those of heaven;
and to share these with others, I was willing to be shut
away as a prisoner.

Thérèse arrived back at Lisieux on December 2, but no
word about her application was received until after
Christmas, and then the news was not entirely satisfactory to her; she was accepted but would have to wait till
Easter time before entering the Carmel. She confessed to
a very human impulse to relax somewhat during that time,
but she dismissed it quickly and continued what she
called her "mortified life" up to the time of her entrance
into the Carmel.

The admission date was set for April 9, and after Mass
in the morning her family accompanied her to the cloister
door. She said her last goodbyes, knelt for her father's
blessing, and stepped through the open door. It clicked
shut behind her, and she was cloistered in Carmel.

A few minutes later she was led to her cell, the monastic room, and Pauline watched her as she inspected the
whitewashed walls, the wooden bed, the squat stool.
Thérèse smiled, and she whispered, audibly: "Now I am
here forever."

CHAPTER IV

EVALUATION

St. Thérèse was fifteen years and three months old when she entered Carmel. She spent only nine and a half years there; thus the major portion of her short life lay behind her on that April day when she stepped behind the cloister door. It should be possible, at this stage of her life, to evaluate her character, to discover the general direction in which her personality was developing—not only because she had lived more than half her life, but chiefly because those fifteen years were for her something beyond the simple, rather carefree time of childhood. Her intelligence had matured early, she had run a full gamut of emotional experiences, and she had for many years been involved in an intensive religious program. The pattern should be clear, and the broad outlines of her character, now permanently established, should be discernible.

The salient question about her character and personality is the frequently discussed issue of whether or not she was a neurotic. It is an unavoidable question, one we must face if we are to have any success in a search for St. Thérèse.

1. SAINT AND NEUROTIC?

St. Thérèse is a canonized saint of the Catholic Church, and it is in this light we must view her—a person whose heroic virtue is approved by the Church in an official act. The fundamental question, therefore, is whether a saint, *any* canonized saint could possibly have been a neurotic or psychotic. We must prescind from the readily admitted fact that a neurotic can lead an intense spiritual life, indeed attain some degree of holiness; our only interest, as far as Thérèse is concerned, is whether such a person can practice heroic virtue, can be considered canonizable.

The *Super Dubio* decree of 1921 raises the issue of Thérèse's childhood illness and states that "it exercised so malignant a power upon herself and her actions as to cast suspicion on her sanctity, and seriously to disturb that which is the natural foundation of all heroic virtue." The statement is somewhat obscure, but the phrase, "the natural foundation of all heroic virtue," can obviously mean only one thing.

Pope Pius XII, in 1952, made one of the clearest and most definite statements ever issued by a Pope about the relationship between sanctity and mental illness:

That mental health is one of the fundamental goods from the viewpoint of nature is obvious. But, it is just as clear that such health is also fundamental in the religious and supernatural sphere. In fact, the full development of religious values and of Christian sanctity in a soul is inconceivable if a man does not start out with a healthy mind, well balanced in its activities.[1]

This official statement of the Pope, which was published in the *Acta*, represents the present view of the Holy See on the issue, and places it in the category of those doctrines to which we must give "religious assent." The statement is explicit: "Christian sanctity in a soul is inconceivable if a man does not start out with a healthy mind, well balanced in its activities." The Pope, therefore, denies that it is possible for a canonized saint to be a neurotic or psychotic, and his words stand in sharp conflict with those who hold that inadmissable theory. No debate on the Pope's statement is necessary: it is clear, it is emphatic, and it closes the discussion.

An interesting footnote to the question is offered by Father Gabriel of St. Mary Magdalen, O.C.D., who for many years before his death was a consultor of the Congregation of Rites and worked on innumerable causes of canonization. He writes:

> From the point of view of causes of beatification, doubt concerning the existence in a servant of God of some such trouble [psychical unbalance] is not a sufficient reason for immediately rejecting the cause: a very careful examination of the doubt is made. It is not actually possible to find a case in which proceedings have afterwards been continued. I could, on the other hand, point to some causes set aside because of doubts of this nature which were not satisfactorily resolved.[2]

Here we have, in Father Gabriel's explanation, the actual practice of the Congregation regarding causes for beatification in which there is *even a doubt* about the possibility of some mental imbalance: such causes are always discontinued and the candidate never beatified.

An American psychologist, Richard Vaughan. S.J., has offered a penetrating analysis of the reason why a neurotic could not possibly practice the heroic virtue demanded for canonization.[3] Father Vaughan outlines some of the fundamental aspects of a neurotic personality

—self-centeredness, anger and hostility in dealing with others, inability to have concern for values beyond himself—and contrasts these with the concept of heroic virtue. Heroic virtue, particularly the virtue of charity, demands an altruism, an outgoing from self, a genuine concern for others. The neurotic, pathetically involved in himself, simply cannot maintain the evenness of disposition, the gentle charity, the self-forgetfulness required of heroic virtue. "In view of our analysis of the seriously neurotic personality," Father Vaughan concludes, "it is difficult to see how a religious could attain all the aforesaid virtues to a heroic degree, and thus be worthy of canonization."

We seem to be, therefore, in possession of conclusive and incontrovertible arguments that the Holy See does not admit the possibility of neurosis in a canonized saint, and does not, in fact, even beatify those about whom it harbors a doubt. These *a priori* arguments should help us in making an accurate conclusion about St. Thérèse.

2. A NEUROTIC THÉRÈSE?

Father Robo summarizes his evaluation of Thérèse: "St. Teresa was a nervous subject; she may be called a neuropath; she suffered from psychoneurosis" (p. 234). In his estimation, her mental imbalance was an infirmity which lasted until her death; indeed, he makes the startling statement that it was employed as a way to achieve sanctity:

To the praise of St. Thérèsa, let us point out that a weakness which is usually a lifelong handicap was conquered by her as far as one can conquer an incurable infirmity, and that she made an unexpected use of it as the means of reaching sanctity. (p. 238)

The instant question is how such an evaluation, so obviously in conflict with the thought of the Holy See, could ever be made. The answer must assuredly be that the new critics are reading the facts of Thérèse's life in a different way than the Holy See, and are interpreting these facts by a different norm, a different yardstick. One childhood episode of St. Thérèse, frequently quoted as an indication of her neurosis, might serve as an example.

In the autobiography, Thérèse tells of her fishing expeditions with her father when they would walk out into the country carrying a basket lunch until they reached some stream where they spent the afternoon. Thérèse fished with a small rod of her own, and she sometimes just sat on the bank, praying. "My thoughts were quite deep," she wrote, "and although I knew nothing of how to meditate, my soul was sunk deep into a state of genuine prayer." When it came time to open the basket Pauline had prepared for them, she discovered that the sandwiches had become soggy as the jam ran through the bread. "Then this world seemed an even sadder place to me, and I knew that only in heaven would there be joy without shadows." Frau Goerres sees this as an example of her "melancholy":

> . . . certainly, mysterious and sudden fits of melancholy on the part of children are fairly common. Nevertheless, such sadness over—of all things—a stale jam sandwich must strike us as strange. (p. 63)

Unwittingly, Goerres and the other critics have placed their fingers on the crux of a stern problem which reaches even beyond the limits of St. Thérèse's case: the so-called problem of discernment of spirits, or better, the problem of judging the validity of a religious experience. If we see a girl of Thérèse's age involved in an intensive religious program, we might have our doubts as to whether it is really a valid and genuine program, or whether perhaps it is an unhealthy withdrawal from the real world. Here is a child who, even before she reaches her tenth birthday, is thinking of serious and adult religious concepts, who is practicing a continuing series of mortifications, who is devoting more and more time to prayer and less and less time to the ordinary pursuits of childhood. Sanctity or abnormality? This is the crucial problem which spiritual directors and confessors are often asked to answer, and it is one of the most perplexing problems to solve. Very often a spiritual director, confused and uncertain, can only make a hesitant guess at the actual time of direction, and only the passage of time supplies any real solution as one gains the infallible vision of hindsight.

But—the vital point!—in the case of Thérèse Martin we do have that hindsight, we do know where her religious program was leading her. Her practices of solitude and mortification and prolonged prayer—yes, even her realization that a stale jam sandwich epitomized the failure of all earthly things—were leading her to a greater perfection, to a fuller friendship with God, and ultimately to canonization as a saint of the universal Church. Why must we limit ourselves to wondering about whether a girl's preoccupation with a jam sandwich and her growing fervor were abnormal or not when we can view the whole spectrum of her life, when we have the opportunity of seeing the ultimate result of these early tendencies? This limited viewpoint and evaluation is the unhappy product when a biographer confines himself to psychology, to a one-dimensional view of a saint. There is another dimension—that of divine grace, abiding in the saint and providing a new life, a new impulse.

All Thérèse's biographers will admit she was an extremely religious girl; but that is not enough. She was more than just extremely religious, she was extraordinarily and unusually religious, much more than the average girl. Abbé Domin, her confessor and teacher at the abbey, remembers questioning her about her prayer when she was ten or twelve, and said he believed her prayer at that young age was a truly contemplative prayer. Pauline recalls a little notebook she gave Thérèse some three months before her first Communion for marking her mortifications and prayer, and when Pauline inspected the book on her Communion day there were carefully noted 818 sacrifices and 2774 acts or aspirations of love. (This practice of spiritual tabulation might be disputed as far too mechanical, although it is still being employed even in many American convents and monasteries, but it does provide the historian with splendid documentary evidence.) We are dealing, therefore, with someone who is inhabiting a high plane of religious living; and this fact should be thoughtfully considered as we attempt to evaluate Thérèse.

A number of eminent spiritual theologians—Garrigou-LaGrange, Marie-Eugene, Gabriel of St. Mary Magdalene, among them[4]—have duly noted the full dimension of St. Thérèse, the spiritual as well as the historical aspect, and have concluded that her early behavior pattern is a clear example of God's grace elevating a soul to a higher level of perfection. For them, there is no psychological abnormality, but rather normality being led to sanctity.

In God's plan, sanctity and perfection are not achieved through an instantaneous act, despite the new religious values which might be acquired through a "conversion" or "experience." In the supernatural life, as well as in the natural life, there must be growth, development, progress until the individual arrives at some degree of sanctity. This is the most profound meaning of the many

parables Christ tells in which He compares grace in a
man's soul to seed placed in the ground: the seed must
grow and mature; it must take root in good ground and
not be stifled by thorns, as Christ states in the parable of
the sower and the seed.[5] We must, in the language of
St. Paul, "grow up in Him who is Christ." But this demands a process of spiritual maturation, a continuing
change, which has to be accompanied by effort, travail,
suffering. Christ tells us that we must inhere in Him as
branches to a vine, and His Father will be the vinedresser
who will accomplish this process. "Every branch in me
that beareth not fruit, he will take away; and every one
that beareth fruit, he will purge it, that it may bring
forth more fruit."[6] This *purge* of which Christ speaks
is the process God employs to lead the soul to a greater
union with Him and to divest it even further of self-inter-
est and self-love. But the capital point in spiritual growth
is that the soul not only works toward union with God,
but that God Himself operates on the soul, preparing it,
elevating it, and purging it. This process has been described frequently by saints and spiritual writers, but no
one has delineated it with more eloquence, more clarity,
than St. John of the Cross, a Doctor of the Church.

In St. John of the Cross' doctrine, God conducts the
soul through two "nights," in order to purge it and lead
it to union with Him. After an initial period of endeavor
in which the soul conceives a strong love for God, makes
a firm commitment to Him, and begins to detach itself of
all things for Him, God sends the first night, the "night of
the senses" in St. John of the Cross' terminology. The
night of the senses might last years, or even decades,
until it terminates in a period of peace and close union
with God. If a soul is to be elevated to the highest form of
union, God then conducts it through the night of the
spirit, a more difficult and more painful purgation. The

termination point of the second night is complete union with God, or spiritual espousals, or any of the other names by which it is known.

The theologians cited above claim that Thérèse was being conducted along these paths, that God introduced her into the "nights" for the purpose of raising her to complete union with Him. This is an evaluation which seems to correspond perfectly with the pattern of her life. As a young girl, she began a determined program of giving herself completely to God ("From the age of three I refused the good God nothing"), and did everything she possibly could to please Him. God then plunged her into a long period of suffering, the night of the senses according to this evaluation. During that night she continued her efforts to please God, but there were problems, difficulty, travail—God was purging her. Her "conversion" at Christmas, 1886, was the dramatic termination of the night of the senses, and introduced her into a closer union with God and a more vital desire of working for Him. After she entered Carmel, she passed through another and more difficult trial, a painful aridity and desolation in prayer, an inability to perceive any consolation in her contact with God—the night of the spirit. When she emerged from that period, she was in the highest stages of the spiritual life, the spiritual espousals; and shortly afterwards, she experienced her "mystical wounding" of 1895. The last eighteen months of her life, she endured her temptations against faith which were apparently a period of suffering for souls and the Church, a direct response to her oblation to God's love, in June of 1895.

This is an evaluation of her life which takes into account the factor of divine grace in her soul and which leaves room for God's purifying action. It ratifies what Dom Godfrey Madelaine, her advisor and occasional confessor during her last years, said of her at the trial:

In reading her life, one is amazed by the truly small number of extraordinary happenings which are related. I believe that her life was, in actuality, very simple and that extraordinary things were rare, at least as far as external manifestations are concerned. But her interior life is an entirely different thing. My conversations with her and my study of her writings force me to believe she had been elevated by God to the highest degrees of the life of union. I read St. Teresa's writings again on this subject in *The Interior Castle* and was stunned that the description she gives of the highest states corresponds exactly with what I have observed in the Servant of God.

Thérèse, therefore, reached complete union with God, and she assuredly must have obtained it according to the traditional process described by spiritual writers through the ages. Hence, if we view her life in that aspect, we are not watching a neurotic girl, but rather a soul being conducted by God's purifying action.

The facts by which Thérèse's neurosis is supposedly proved are unconvincing and inconclusive. In the autobiography, Thérèse includes a letter written by her mother in which Mme. Martin recounts some temper tantrums of the two-year-old child, and concludes: "She is a very nervous child." (Literally, *C'est une enfant bien nerveuse.* Knox translates *nerveuse* as "excitable.") What Mme. Martin meant by "nervous" must be studied in the light of another letter Thérèse quotes a few pages later in the autobiography: her mother relates how Céline would take her baby sister with her when she left the house for some art lessons, and Thérèse would sit quietly during the lessons, "not moving at all for two or three hours." We see extraordinary control in a girl of two years, indications that she was not quite as nervous as some of her biographers have painted her.

Thérèse's tears are alleged as another "proof" of her neuroticism. The witnesses at the trial stated that the great majority of her crying spells were caused by her concern for having offended either God or some acquaintance; and while that, of course, does not explain her propensity for tears, because we know many times she cried unreasonably, it does provide us some insight to the situation. Admittedly, this was a fault in the young girl. Thérèse herself deplored it and tried to correct it, but only her Christmas conversion of 1886 gave her mastery. But does the frequent weeping of an affectionate and sensitive girl prove she is a neurotic? Would we automatically consider a small girl neurotic if she is prone to tears when things go against her? It would hardly seem so.

These facts—her supposed nervousness, her tears, her alleged melancholy, and a few other similar episodes— are the materials out of which a neurotic Thérèse is constructed. In opposition, we have the careful studies of eminent theologians (like Garrigou-LaGrange and Marie-Eugene) and of priest-psychiatrists (like Verner Moore and Raphael Simon) asserting that Thérèse was not neurotic, that instead she was being conducted through the "nights" to a complete union with God.

A succinct account of Thérèse's interior life, from the viewpoint of psychology and spiritual theology, is offered by the Trappist psychiatrist, Father Raphael Simon, O.C.S.O., and he concludes his study:

In this account of St. Thérèse's spiritual life her experiences have not been reduced to neurotic phenomena, in ignorance of both mystical theology and psychiatry, as has been attempted . . . I am convinced that any competent clinical psychiatrist who examined

Thérèse in life, would have marveled at the exquisite balance of her mind, emotions, and conduct, and would have considered her eminently normal, and of this her autobiography—not only as edited by Mother Agnes, but also as it appears in her original manuscript —is a witness.[7]

This opinion—formed by a competent psychiatrist, written with an understanding of spiritual theology, and completely in harmony with the position of the Holy See about the possibility of a neurotic saint—would seem to be the only adequate one.

CHAPTER V

CARMEL

1. THE RUE DE LIVEROT

The Carmelite convent on the Rue de Liverot (now, the Rue de Carmel) had been founded in 1831, and at the time of Thérèse's entrance it contained twenty-five nuns. The internal life of the Carmel with its interplay of personal relationships and its enigmatic superioress has provided the situation in which a number of commentators have attempted to find some drama and pathos in the hitherto rather drab and commonplace life of the young saint. The raw material for such a presentation was certainly present in the Lisieux Carmel: Mother Marie Gonzague, the prioress, was a difficult person, mercurial in temperament, jealous and ambitious, anxiously guarding her position of authority; some of the other nuns were far from attractive personalities; and the Martin sisters themselves—Pauline and Marie had preceded Thérèse to the Carmel, and Céline was to follow six years later—were regarded suspiciously by some of the nuns as forming a family bloc within the community. St. Thérèse's position in the community and her reaction to the real situation have been submitted to a variety of interpretations. She has been presented as the victim of Mother Gonzague's tyranny, persecuted and opposed throughout her life, and denied proper medical care in her last illness. Some have pictured her as thoroughly shocked by conditions in the Carmel and regretful of her decision to enter that particular convent. Others have seen her as an outcast in the Carmel, disliked by the great majority of the nuns and driven firmly into the small circle of the four Martin sisters. Here again, careful and calm investigation is required to ascertain the rhythm of St. Thérèse's life in Carmel and her relationships to her associates.

Carmel, reaching back in its traditions to the solitaries of Mount Carmel in Palestine, carries the desert into the city by establishing hermitages, places of prayer and penance and solitude, in the midst of urban life. A convent of cloistered Carmelite nuns, therefore, contains a group of women who have voluntarily locked themselves away for the purpose of occupying themselves unremittingly with the things of God. When St. Teresa of Avila founded her first convent of Discalced Carmelite nuns at Avila in 1562 she had a precise goal in mind: as she said in her *Way of Perfection,* she lamented that Christ had so few friends, and she wanted these few friends, at least, to be good friends of His. Preoccupation with God, and prayer for the Church and souls—these were the aims of Carmel.

St. Teresa's first convent, San José in Avila, was the origin of a continuing series of new foundations. By the time of her death in 1582, there were eighteen convents in Spain, and soon afterwards an even wider expansion began, until today there are almost a thousand convents throughout the world. Carmel spread to all parts of Europe, to Asia, Africa, the New World; to large cities and small—even to a small Norman town of Lisieux in a red-bricked building on the Rue de Liverot.

Thérèse's personal objectives were already the same as those of Carmel (she once wrote to her sister Céline: "We have only one thing to do here below—to love Jesus, and save souls for Him that he might be more loved"). But she now had to organize her objectives in the framework and schedule of conventual life. She rose each morning at five o'clock (at six in the winter), made an hour of mental prayer with the nuns in choir, chanted the Little Hours of the Divine Office, and assisted at the conventual Mass. After a breakfast of bread and coffee, she was employed in one of the many household tasks assigned the nuns: immediately after her entrance, she worked in the laundry for nine months; when she received the religious habit at her formal investiture, she was made refectorian, a position she held for two years; then she was employed in art work for a year, painting frescoes, ornaments for the altar, and even some pictures which were sold outside the convent; in 1893 she was made portress; and in 1896 she was placed in charge of the sacristy. She always wanted to become infirmarian and tend the sick nuns, but her desire was never fulfilled.

The main meal of the day was at eleven o'clock, usually consisting of fish, since the Carmelites do not eat meat in their convents, except in the case of illness. An hour of recreation followed, during which the nuns ordinarily did some light work, sewing or weaving or making rosary beads. Vespers were chanted at two o'clock, followed by spiritual reading. There was another hour of mental prayer at five o'clock in the afternoon; then supper, and another recreation period, and the chanting of Compline at seven-thirty. At nine o'clock, the night office, Matins and Lauds, was chanted, and the nuns retired about eleven.

From her first day in the convent, Thérèse applied herself vigorously to this new form of life. She took an im-

mediate position in regard to her sisters Pauline and
Marie, a position which seemed to surprise even them: she
made it quite clear that, despite her natural feelings, she
was not going to continue the life of Les Buissonnets in
Carmel. She tried to treat her sisters with no greater attention or friendship than that which she bestowed on the
other nuns; it was an heroic stand, one requiring a constant sacrifice for the affectionate fifteen-year-old girl.
Three weeks after her entrance, Marie stopped her to explain how to use the breviary for that day's Office. Thérèse
smiled and said she had already arranged her breviary
and would not need any help. "I would love to stop and
speak with you a while," she told her sister, "but I must
deprive myself of that, for we are no longer at home."
Thérèse herself relates an episode in her autobiography
when she desperately wanted to chat with Pauline, who
was then prioress; no one certainly would have objected
to a nun talking with her superior, but still Thérèse
wanted to deny herself this satisfaction and actually had
to run past the door of Pauline's cell to stifle her natural
impulse.

Her determination to live the Carmelite life with the
greatest amount of honesty and fidelity did not go unnoticed by her superiors. Mother Marie Gonzague, the
prioress, wrote about her in a letter shortly after her entrance: "Never would I have believed that a child of fifteen could possess such mature judgement; there is nothing to criticize in her, everything is perfect." Her novice
mistress, Mother Marie of the Angels, who stated at the
trial that she knew Thérèse better than anyone else during the early period of her religious life, said:

She had an extraordinary comprehension of sanctity
and the religious life and the sacrifices it demands. She
put herself to the task of sanctity with a firm courage

which never recoiled from any obstacle. I never noticed any imperfection in this dear child all the time she was in the novitiate. And during the fifteen years I was novice mistress, no novice I ever had equalled her in perfection and virtue.

The novice mistress also recalled that an elderly sister in the convent spoke to her in admiration about Thérèse's period in the novitiate: "Truly, we have never seen anything like that before!"

This testimony gives an indication of her basic and initial approach to conventual life. Thérèse's life in Carmel was marked with the same fervor and religious generosity as her earlier years. She was unswerving in her fidelity to the Rule, she obeyed promptly all the commands issued to her, she was tireless in her acts of charity and kindness to the other nuns. Her sanctity was achieved, however, in a quiet, unobtrusive manner—so much so, in fact, that after her death some of the nuns testified that they had noticed nothing extraordinary in her character or conduct. She followed the austere and simple routine of the Carmelite life with its long hours of prayer, its fasts and abstinence, its solitude, its mortifications, and its manual labor.

But Thérèse quickly discovered that a convent is composed of more than rules, schedule, organization, and laws; it is composed of human beings—and human beings, even those in convents, are not always as predictable and perfect as we would like them to be. This was especially true of the nuns in the Carmel of Lisieux. Despite the calm and placid exterior of the building, there was ferment, unrest in the convent. And the trouble all swirled around the enigmatic figure of Mother Marie Gonzague, the prioress.

2. MOTHER MARIE GONZAGUE

As Tolstoy notes in the beginning of his *Anna Karenina*, every happy family is usually happy in much the same way, but every unhappy family is unhappy in its own particular way. During the nine years Thérèse lived in the convent, her religious family of Carmel was, to some extent, an unhappy family; and it is, therefore, almost impossible to reconstruct with any certainty the particular tensions, the particular hostilities, and the particular problems which existed in it. We know a number of different facts and events which occurred at the same time and in the same place, but it is difficult to determine precisely how these situations interplayed on each other to produce the precise rhythm of life in the Lisieux Carmel.

During the first of the two trials for Thérèse's beatification, Mother Marie Gonzague's name began to appear frequently in the testimony, and in an unfavorable light. The ecclesiastical judges, sensing they had stumbled on a real situation influencing Thérèse's life, started to probe more deeply, asking more penetrating questions about the Carmelite prioress. In the second trial, the apostolic process, Pauline introduced a three-thousand-word document which was read into the testimony. This document, an intimate portrayal of Mother Gonzague's character (*un document de communaute*, Pauline called it) was signed by five contemporaries of the prioress. At first reading, the document seems rather petty, a rehash of old grievances, but it does give an amazing and disturbing picture of Mother Gonzague and the upset she caused in the convent.

Marie-Adèle Davy de Virville, a native of Caen, entered the convent on September 29, 1860, at the age of twenty-six, adopting the name Marie de Gonzague. She came from a cultured and refined family. She was tall, carried herself with an air of distinction, and possessed a rich and resonant voice. She was pious, and her superiors commended her for candor and honesty. But serious defects were apparent, too: she was mercurial in temperament, and suffered rapid changes of mood, passing from gaiety to deep melancholy in a matter of moments; she was jealous, and gave way to frequent outbursts of temper and was involved in some violent scenes. At the end of her novitiate, the superior of the Carmel, Abbé Cagniard, expressed grave concern about her and reluctantly ratified the community's decision to accept her vows, hoping her defects would remedy themselves over the years. Pauline's document says, simply and significantly: "That was a fatal error."

The document cites a number of bizarre episodes stretching over many years. (These incidents were first presented to the English-speaking world by John Beevers in his *Storm of Glory,* and he recounts them soberly and honestly.) There is an occasion when, as a younger nun, a fit of jealousy caused her to hide in a corner of the cloister garden for a whole day; after she was found, she was led to the prioress' cell, but when confronted with her superior she had to be restrained from throwing herself out of the window (*au premier étage,* the document notes; that is, from the second story). After her election as prioress, these unfortunate incidents multiplied. She became even more possessive, demanding an intense personal loyalty and devotion from the nuns of the community. She allowed the nuns to receive Communion—something which lay within the discretion of the superior at that time—according to the amount of personal attachment they had for her; once she even allowed Communion as a reward to a nun who had trapped a rat for her pet cat.

She was unsympathetic with the sick, stating imperiously: "There are sicknesses today which people never even heard of before, and it is sinful to nurse them." Each year during the annual retreat, she maintained a surveillance over the confessional, counting the time each nun spent in consultation with the priest.

In her own personal life, Mother Marie Gonzague spent a long time every day in the convent parlor with a lady of the town who brought her all the local gossip; and, in turn, she carried these trivial, worldly stories to the nuns' recreation periods. Her sister, a countess, was a frequent visitor at the convent; she remained, of course, in the guest lodgings outside the cloister, but the nuns of the community were forced to wait on her, washing her linens, doing embroidering and lace work for her. Whenever the countess arrived, a sigh of desperation passed around the community—"Ah, Madame is here!" The convent had to lend her money, and it paid for doctor's fees when she was ill.

Yet, Mother Gonzague was elected and re-elected to the office of prioress by the free balloting of the community. A prioress is elected for a three-year term, and can be re-elected for another three years, after which she becomes ineligible until someone else holds the office for a time; however, the bishop can dispense with that rule, as he often did in Mother Gonzague's case. She was first elected in 1874, re-elected in 1877, and then the bishop continued her term of office until 1883. The same process was duplicated when she was prioress for 1886 until 1893. Pauline, now Mother Agnes, was elected prioress in 1893, but Mother Gonzague returned for two more terms in 1896. She finished her last term in 1902, and died of cancer of the tongue in 1904.

Pauline was Mother Gonzague's personal choice for the

office in 1893, because she felt she could manipulate her while she was forced into temporary retirement. But she made a poor selection, for Pauline soon showed she wanted to govern the community on a more intelligent and equitable basis, and she refused to be managed by her former superior. Mother Gonzague, who possessed the title of novice mistress, proceeded to make life difficult for Pauline, opposing her, contradicting her in public. Before the elections of 1896, she began a campaign among the nuns to frustrate Mother Agnes' re-election; she was successful, but only after a long and painful election in which she gained victory on the seventh ballot. The community thus found itself divided into two camps, those who supported Mother Gonzague for prioress, and those who supported Pauline. This was the cause of even greater anxiety within the community, and Abbé Jouf, the chaplain for over twenty-five years, said to a nun one day: "Is it not tragic that souls believing they will find simplicity in Carmel, are forced to play at politics."

These are the grim aspects of Mother Gonzague's character and the harm she caused the community. There is, however, another side to the coin. She did possess a fantastic amount of charm and was able to attract people to herself easily; she succeeded in having a new addition built on the convent; she did give sound advice to the nuns who approached her, although it was necessary to flatter her to gain her attention. And there is the undeniable fact that she was constantly being elected prioress in the free elections of the community which were presided over by the bishop or a priest delegated by him. This latter fact raises the inevitable question: Why did the nuns constantly re-elect her as prioress? A number of answers suggest themselves. Perhaps her faults did not seem as grievous when considered in the total context of her personality and contrasted with the good qualities we know she possessed; and thus perhaps the nuns at Lisieux, living in the real situation, were not quite as horrified by Mother Gonzague's faults as we are today when we take them and examine them one by one. Or perhaps, as so often happens in female religious communities, the nuns were looking for a strong and forceful personality as an administrator. Or perhaps, in the most profound explanation, Mother Gonzague's attractive and magnetic personality was able to make the nuns disregard or minimize her faults; and if this was the case, we find ourselves presented with one of those not unusual and enigmatic situations of human nature when we can love and cherish a person even though he possesses serious faults and defects.

Dom Godfrey Madelaine, the prior of a Premonstratensian Abbey, was well acquainted with the Lisieux Carmel, and he was asked at the trial for an evaluation of Mother Gonzague. His reply is interesting and informative:

I knew her well. I had many visits with her in the parlor, and we corresponded frequently. She seemed to have particularly good judgement. In the administration of the community she was intent on doing what was right. Judging by my own association with her, I felt her character was excellent. It is impossible for me to evaluate her conduct in the intimate life of the cloister. Her numerous re-elections to the office of prioress seem to argue that the nuns appreciated her method of government. She confided to me that there was a clash of personality between her and Mother Agnes, and they made each other suffer despite a very sincere mutual esteem for each other. But in these confidences there was no hint of bitterness.

Dom Madelaine's testimony gives us another view of Mother Gonzague, or at least it shows the face she was able to wear for outsiders.

Thérèse's relationship to this strange woman who was her superior for most of the time she was in the Carmel has been the object of much speculation. The most frequent modern evaluation depicts the prioress as a Torquemada or a Cauchon intent on persecuting the young nun. However, this is too dramatic and too simple a presentation, one not supported by the evidence. Two equally undeniable sets of facts must somehow be correlated to obtain the true picture. First, Mother Gonzague did treat Thérèse harshly during her early days in the convent. Dom Madelaine testified, "The prioress acted toward her with a severity that seemed excessive." And Thérèse, herself, wrote in the autobiography that Mother Gonzague was very severe in dealing with her (*très sévère* she wrote, and she underlined the first word twice and the second word three times). Thérèse recounted that almost every time she met her superior she would be corrected for something she had done inadequately. Once when Thérèse had failed to notice a cobweb hanging in a corridor she had cleaned, the prioress upbraided her before the whole community. And when the novice mistress sent her to work in the garden during the afternoon, the prioress taunted her for the easy and agreeable assignment she had been given.

However, as Frau Goerres has correctly noted, Mother Gonzague's attitude toward Thérèse was not dictated by pique or dissatisfaction with her; rather, this was her method of training the exceptional person she found her to be. There are numerous references in the testimony at the trial noting the high regard Mother Gonzague had for Thérèse: she worked diligently to obtain her early entrance; the letters she wrote to outsiders are filled with praise for her; and Dom Madelaine remembers she always spoke of her as "my little angel." Even the document Mother Agnes read into the record admits that the prioress had a sincere affection and admiration for Thérèse.

One might dispute the wisdom of such pedagogy, but one cannot dispute the purity of Mother Gonzague's intentions. Writing about this matter, Thérèse stated: "What a priceless grace! Certainly, God was acting visibly through this person who was taking His place on earth. What would have become of me if, as people outside thought, I had become the pet of the community?" Actually, given her initial dispositions in the convent, there was little danger of that, but still Mother Gonzague made sure that it would be impossible by continually upbraiding the young nun and finding fault with her. It was a trial by fire, but the prioress was convinced that this unusual soul—of whom she wrote, "everything about her is perfect"—should be trained that way.

Even more amazing is Thérèse's reaction to her prioress: she was one of the many people who became attracted and fascinated by this charming, yet tyrannical woman. Mother Marie of the Angels testified that Thérèse had to fight against becoming unduly attached to the prioress. And Pauline said: "She confided to me that she truly loved Mother Marie de Gonzague, and that the expressions 'My beloved mother' and 'My dearest mother' which I found in her memoirs really expressed the true sentiments of her heart." However, her affection for the prioress was not a blind one; she recognized the woman's faults, and Marie even remembers that Thérèse asked her to pray that Mother Gonzague might correct herself. Yet the strange fascination endured, and as the years passed the prioress became more and more dependent on Thérèse, confiding in her, asking her help. An eloquent proof of this new relationship is the note Thérèse wrote her su-

perior after the community elections of 1886. Mother
Gonzague was thoroughly shaken when she needed seven
ballots to be elected, and Thérèse's daring note, an alle-
gory about a lamb and the Good Shepherd, attempts to
console the prioress and elevate her thinking to a more
spiritual level.

Pauline assisted Mother Gonzague as she lay dying in
1904, and the former prioress said, somewhat pathetically: "My mother, I could not hope to be saved if I did
not have my little Thérèse interceding for me; I feel I owe
my salvation to her."

There are many nuances to Mother Gonzague's relationship with the community of Lisieux, and perhaps it
was Mother Marie of the Angels who best summarized
the situation at the trial: "The Servant of God, with her
remarkable cleverness, knew well the serious defects
which were joined to the beautiful qualities in that
Mother whom we loved despite everything else."

3. THÉRÈSE AND THE COMMUNITY

Whatever other qualities Mother Gonzague may have
had, she lacked the necessary abilities for leadership and
government. She played favorites, she made her own
moods and feelings the basis of decisions for the community, she lacked the calm, the forbearance, the meekness
required for successful government of a religious order,
and she allowed that most invidious of all things to occur
—a division within the community, a spirit of party which
saw the convent split into irreconcilable groups. One
group of nuns, most of them the older members of the
community, rallied around her; and the other group,
composed chiefly of the younger nuns, supported Pauline,
seeing in her the answer to Carmel's problems. This divi-

sion within the Lisieux Carmel lasted until St. Thérèse's
death and greatly influenced the reaction of some nuns
toward her. Despite Thérèse's successful determination to
disassociate herself from her family background in the
convent, some of the nuns could not help but automatically classify her as a member of the group supporting her
sister Pauline. This is the sentiment behind the rather
amusing statement that Sister Marie of the Trinity testified she heard Mother Gonzague make a number of
times: "If I had to choose a prioress from this community,
I would unhesitatingly choose Sister Thérèse of the Infant Jesus, despite her youth. She is perfect in all aspects,
and her only fault is having three sisters here in the convent with her."

Thérèse could have reacted to the division within the
community in any one of three ways: she could have
sided with her sister, she could have become a part of
Mother Gonzague's faction, or she could have lived above
the whole situation, minding her own business, siding
with neither party. This latter course was the one she
chose. She refused to become involved in the internal
strife of the community and sedulously avoided any discussion of the issues. A current interpretation of the Carmelite constitutions made this somewhat easy to accomplish: according to that interpretation, no more than two
blood sisters could vote in the community elections, or
even be present at the business meetings of the house
chapter. Thus, for all practical purposes, Thérèse remained a novice all the time she lived in the convent,
someone living within the community, but not a voting
member of the convent government. But the principal reason for her position of withdrawal from controversy was
her fine perception of the basic purposes of conventual
life. At the trial, Marie commented on Thérèse's position
in Carmel:

I am obliged to say that during the years Sister Thérèse was in the Carmel of Lisieux, this community was forced to undergo regrettable disturbances: there were opposing factions, and defects of character, the principal one being the peevish temperament of Mother Gonzague, who held the office of prioress at different times over a twenty-year span. In this troubled environment, the Servant of God's prudence and virtue were demonstrated in a truly remarkable manner. In the middle of all the tumult, she was able to avoid all species of conflict and never allowed her union with God to disappear, nor her search for perfection, nor her love for all the sisters, nor her respect for authority.

Sister Aimée was a member of the faction which supported Mother Gonzague, and she at first resented Thérèse, whom she thought must certainly be a supporter of her sister; only gradually did she realize that Thérèse had no interest in the politics of the convent. She testified:

I was one of the instruments with which God sanctified her, since by charitably enduring my faults she reached a higher degree of sanctity. Her charity toward her neighbor was disinterested and supernatural. Her conduct toward the chapter sisters was, it seemed to me, heroic when Mother Agnes barely received enough votes to be elected. The secrecy of the balloting was not very well preserved, and Thérèse showed no animosity toward those who voted against her sister.

The witnesses testified that Thérèse could be observed making a careful effort to avoid an entanglement with either faction, particularly with the group supporting Pauline, to which she must certainly have been attracted both because of her personal devotion to her sister and because of Pauline's sensible administration. When she found some nuns whispering to each other in the corridor—an infraction of the rules—she would smile pleasantly, nod her head, and move gracefully on. At recreation she deliberately sat near the nuns opposed to her sister, talking with them cheerfully and pleasantly. When she was novice mistress she sternly forbade any criticism of Mother Gonzague (the novices, characteristically, had devised a nickname for the prioress—"the wolf") and promptly silenced any public discussions of the situation.

Her attitude during this unpleasant situation which endured for her whole life in Carmel shows, perhaps more than anything else, her maturity and her amazing self-control.

Was Thérèse liked by the nuns in the convent?—this was the question asked by the judges at the trial. The witnesses make some careful distinctions. The nuns all considered her a good little nun, somewhat reserved, very charitable, and absolutely faithful to the rule and constitutions. Sister Aimée testified, however, that some of the nuns did not realize the full extent of her holiness until after her death because of the quiet and hidden pattern of her life. "Nevertheless," she added, "I can testify that during her lifetime all the nuns considered her an exceptionally virtuous soul, especially remarkable for her humility, her charity, and her kindness." That was the general tenor of the testimony: those who knew Thérèse well considered her a person of amazing sanctity, but those who were not too well acquainted with her felt she was just a good nun. Thus, one of her novices, Sister Mary Magdalene, testified: "The novices were very well aware of her sanctity, but about half the community felt she was just a good little religious, very sweet, but one who never had anything real to suffer and whose life was somewhat insignificant."

Interestingly enough, Thérèse enjoyed a greater reputation for sanctity among people outside the convent than among those with whom she lived. This was due to the reports carried outside by the priests she consulted—the retreat masters, the chaplain, the confessors—and to the glowing accounts transmitted to visitors by her superiors, Mother Gonzague and Mother Marie of the Angels. All of the outside witnesses who appeared at the trial were unanimous in their assertions that the young nun was considered to be extraordinarily holy, even during her lifetime. A somewhat amusing illustration of the axiom, "The exception proves the rule," was offered at the trial by Abbé Domin, the chaplain at the abbey school. He complained that there was too much excitement and praise about the young Carmelite nun. One day he paid a visit at the Carmel to his former pupil, and Mother Gonzague praised Thérèse in her presence for her fidelity and generosity; he felt it was wrong to praise a young person in her presence. Again, at the parish of Saint Jacques the Abbé Jouf said to him: "Despite her youth, she could be nominated prioress of the community without any hesitation at all." Abbé Domin commented:

This statement of my confrere seemed to me what the English call "bluff," and the final result was that I did not visit the Carmel to see her very often. I did not speak about her much because I felt her reputation was exaggerated and I did not want to participate in this concert of praise. *Hélas!* I made a mistake in not believing that her virtue was extraordinary; I recognize that now.

The fact that the full extent of her sanctity was recognized only by those who had some close association with her demonstrates two things: first, her virtue was hidden, unostentatious, and calmly woven into the fabric of her daily life; second, her virtue was not sensational and spectacular, but rather something achieved, as Pius XI said, *without going beyond the common order of things.*

But this does not answer our original question: was Thérèse *liked* in the community? For the most part she was, but there were some nuns who did not appreciate her apparent aloofness, her withdrawal from the petty intrigues of the convent, and her unswerving dedication to the rules of the order. Sister Thérèse of St. Augustine summarized this feeling at the trial:

During the lifetime of the Servant of God, I heard different evaluations of her. Those religious who knew her better, especially the novices, admired the sublimity of her virtues. Others just did not notice them because, I believe, of her simplicity. And others formed rather unfavorable judgements of her; they considered her to be cold and haughty. In my estimation, this was because she spoke little and remained recollected and reserved. Also, perhaps the presence of four sisters in the same community aroused some sentiments of jealousy or opposition.

The ecclesiastical judges pursued this subject, inquiring how many nuns felt this way about Thérèse. "Oh, a small number," Sister Thérèse of St. Augustine answered. Were these nuns noted for holiness and intelligence? "They were fervent, or at least so it seemed to me; but as for intelligence, and especially for correct judgement, that is another affair."

This small group in the convent that regarded Thérèse unfavorably was apparently composed of Mother Gonzague's faction; they resented her detachment from the political scene, perhaps regarding it as a silent rebuff. But there is one other cause for this unfavorable reaction, something striking deeply into the problems of human nature and human iniquity. Sister Marie Magdalene commented on it:

Sister Thérèse of the Infant Jesus was constantly doing nice things for those from whom she could not expect either joy or consolation or tenderness. I was one of that number. From the first days of my entrance up until her death, I never felt myself attracted toward her in any emotional way. I fled from her. It was not a lack of esteem on my part; on the contrary, I found her too perfect. Had she been less perfect it would have encouraged me. I do not believe I ever gave her any consolation. However, she did not abandon me because of that; rather, she was very kind toward me. When I was sad she would try to distract me and make me merry. She never stopped trying to do nice things for me in her own discreet way.

"I found her too perfect," Sister Marie Magdalene said, and yet we know that Thérèse was not a forbidding person: she was pleasant and amiable in her associations with the nuns, and the witnesses recount stories of how she would entertain the nuns at recreation with stories and with her imitations and mimicry. Sister Marie Magdalene's attitude can only stem from that strange impulse which sometimes makes people react against holiness in another person. And in this instance we again see the truth of Ralph Waldo Emerson's cryptic statement— "Colleges hate geniuses, just as convents hate saints."

The autobiography affords us some examples of how
Thérèse, on her part, practiced charity toward the nuns
with whom she lived. There is the story of her gentle forbearance of the nun who carelessly splashed her with
water while they were doing the wash; and her patient
endurance of the nun who was fidgeting in chapel, scraping her fingernail along her teeth. But the most illuminating story is the one Thérèse tells of her natural dislike for
one of the nuns:

There is one sister in the community who has a talent
for annoying me in every way. I find her manners, her
words, and her character entirely disagreeable. But she
is a holy religious whom God must love very much. I
was not going to succumb to this natural antipathy, so
I reminded myself that charity does not consist in feelings but in deeds. Therefore, I tried to do for this sister
whatever I would have done for the person I loved best.
Every time I met her I prayed for her, offering to the
good God all her virtues and merits. . . . I tried to ren-
der all the services to her I could and when I had the
temptation to answer her sharply I would put on my
most friendly smile and try to change the conversation.
. . . She was completely unconscious of my real feelings for her and had no suspicion about the true mo-
tives of my conduct; even now, she is convinced that I
find her personality attractive. One day at recreation
she happily asked me something like this: "Tell me,
Sister Thérèse of the Infant Jesus, what is it that you
find so attractive about me, because you always have a
smile for me whenever I look at you?" Ah, Jesus hidden
in her soul was what I found attractive; Jesus, who
makes bitter things sweet. I answered that I smiled because I was happy to see her (of course, I did not explain that my happiness was completely spiritual).

There is a denouement to the story in that the nun—it was Sister Thérèse of St. Augustine—remained convinced, even after Thérèse's death, of the saint's "irresistible attraction" for her; and she refused to believe she was the nun about whom Thérèse had written. It is reassuring to watch a canonized saint struggling against the natural dislikes we all experience from time to time; and her statement that "charity does not consist in feelings but in deeds" is a sobering rearticulation of basic Christian principles.

The witnesses at the trial relate countless stories of Thérèse's constant charity. Céline noticed how she carefully managed to continually meet a nun who had a habit of asking other people to help her with her work; she artfully contrived to be at hand just when the sister was looking for someone to help her. There was another occasion when Thérèse was working in the refectory and a nun tried to assist her by pinning back her scapular: as the nun fastened the scapular over her shoulder, she accidentally pushed the pin through Thérèse's flesh so that the scapular was acutally pinned to her shoulder; Thérèse calmly endured the small pain and waited until the nun had departed before removing the pin. Then there was the old sister who, as Marie said, would try the patience of an angel: she had the habit of lecturing and preaching incessantly to the sister with whom she was working. Thérèse worked with her a number of years, but one day Marie happened to be assigned to a task with her, and the old nun began to annoy her. Marie spoke to her sharply, and the nun said: "Oh, Sister Thérèse of the Infant Jesus never spoke to me like that." Marie discussed it with Thérèse, and her sister told her: "Oh, be nice to her, she is sick. It is charity to let her think that she is doing us some good, and it gives us the opportunity of practicing patience." Marie expressed some amazement to Thérèse at her ability to be kind and tactful even with those who were somewhat difficult. "How will I prove my love for Jesus if I act otherwise?" Thérèse answered.

There is only one incident related in the entire trial which could conceivably be considered a failure of charity on Thérèse's part, and of course, the Devil's Advocate used it in his case. In the early winter of 1896, two of the nuns were due to make their religious profession of vows, Céline and Sister Marie of the Trinity. Pauline was then prioress, but her term expired in March of that year. Mother Gonzague held the title of novice mistress, but she felt sure she would be elected prioress in the March elections and thus wanted the professions postponed until she could officiate at the ceremony. A heated discussion ensued, and the matter was finally presented to the ecclesiastical superior, Abbé Maupas. The Abbé assembled the community in the parlor and firmly stated that the two nuns should be professed in February. The witnesses recalled that Mother Gonzague turned pale, but said nothing until after the priest had departed; then she continued her campaign to have the professions postponed. One day in recreation when Mother Gonzague was absent, the issue was being discussed by the nuns. "After all," one of the nuns said, "the novice mistress is entirely justified in trying these novices." Thérèse, who had remained silent during the whole affair, finally spoke out: "There are some forms of trial—postponing a religious profession out of jealousy, and endangering the loss of a vocation—which no one has a right to impose."

The Devil's Advocate charged Thérèse with a lack of charity and obedience. But the response given in the *Processus* by the ecclesiastical judge, Msgr. Toeschi, praises Thérèse for her zeal and spirit of justice. The response notes that the profession of the two nuns had been approved by the prioress and the ecclesiastical superior, and Mother Gonzague's conduct constituted an act of disobedience; Thérèse's statement, therefore, was an attempt to clarify the issue and place the whole affair in its proper perspective. Furthermore, the two nuns to be professed were under Thérèse's direction, and she did feel some responsibility for them. We can see in the incident one more manifestation of the same kind of courage and forthrightness Thérèse exhibited before Pope Leo XIII in Rome some years before—and Msgr. Toeschi's official response notes that Thérèse took this stand heedless of the fact that if Mother Gonzague were elected prioress, she could punish her.

Eventually, a compromise was reached, and only one of the nuns, Céline, was professed in February, while Sister Marie of the Trinity had to wait until April, after the elections at which Mother Gonzague was indeed elected. Sister Marie of the Trinity testified that she complained to Thérèse about the injustice of this, but all Thérèse could tell her was she had to offer it to God as a sacrifice. The novice, however, had difficulty in accepting it, and confessed she was brooding about the situation a few evenings later when suddenly a strong sense of peace and acceptance flooded her soul. In the morning, she asked Thérèse if she had been praying for her on the previous evening. "Yes," she answered, "I felt myself strangely compelled to do so last evening during the silence period." That was the very hour at which she had achieved her sudden adjustment, Sister Marie testified.

Sister Thérèse of St. Augustine gave a résumé at the trial of the saint's charity; it is a more remarkable statement when we consider that this was the sister for whom Thérèse had a natural dislike:

She was always trying to make the sisters happy, and that for the purpose of pleasing Our Lord. The Servant of God practiced the most exquisite charity in the community life, denying herself constantly to obtain the happiness of the sisters, tolerating them without complaint and without allowing them to see the sufferings caused by the bad will or jealousy of some who failed to recognize her virtue, staying always with them, sweet, amiable, smiling kindly at them, avoiding anything that could offend them, trying to be agreeable to them, and excusing them constantly.

In attempting to evaluate Thérèse's sanctity, it was necessary for the ecclesiastical judges to study her against the actual background in which she lived; thus, many facts and incidents about the intimate life of the Lisieux Carmel had to be examined and openly discussed. Some of those facts are disturbing, some almost scandalous, and it is easy to arrive at a conclusion that the Lisieux Carmel was an odd and bizarre place filled with cranky and querulous women. However, we must remember that the incidents and episodes recounted in the trial, and even those in the autobiography, are events plucked out of the total fabric of the community's life; they are not sufficient for a complete reconstruction of the total rhythm of life in the Lisieux Carmel. More details, more facts, and more testimony are necessary for that.

Admittedly, there were a number of extremely imperfect personalities in the convent: some of them were flagrantly uncharitable, others were demanding and unfeeling, and at least one appears to have been undeniably neurotic. Then there was the problem of the political split in the community, something which intensified during the election time every three years. Added to this are the exposed glimpses of human nature we get, the outbursts of bad humor, the pique, the occasional petty jealousies. And while we would prefer not to see these in a religious community, we must acknowledge, realistically, that they do occur; a religious community is a family, and although it is a family consecrated and dedicated to God, a family whose members are pledged to perfection, it still remains a family with its clashes of personality and its intimate problems. The witnesses at the trial testified under oath and were put in the unusual position of having to recount a number of intimate and personal facts which ordinarily would never have been known outside the family circle. If we contend that the Lisieux Carmel was an odd and scandalous family, we might ask ourselves this question: could not *any* family subjected to such a scrutiny and exposure—with a revelation of the family fights, the divisions, the jealousies, the occasional bad humor—then be considered odd and scandalous?

Whatever evaluation is placed on the emotional life of the community, we should not make the mistake of concluding that the discipline and religious spirit of the convent was lax. Assuredly, the community was not living at the highest peak of religious fervor—there were notable lapses in silence, and too great a liberty was allowed in receiving visitors in the parlors. But, on the other hand, the Carmelite Rule was, in the main, observed. There was the perpetual abstinence from meat, the long fast each year, the hours of mental prayer, the solitude, the mortifications. And Mother Gonzague, regardless of her own conduct, was not one to indulge the nuns with unnecessary creature comforts—witness her uncompromising attitude toward the sick, even in Thérèse's case.

More important than the actual state of affairs in the Lisieux Carmel was Thérèse's reaction to the real situation she discovered. Did she, confronted with the nuns in Carmel, suffer a severe disillusionment, a tragic disappointment that all the nuns were not already saints? Ida Goerres thinks she did:

There is no reason to assume that Thérèse had even the faintest foreknowledge of these conditions. Indeed, it is improbable, given her pure and unconditional thirst for saintliness, that she would have chosen this convent if she had known. (p. 205)

Goerres speaks of Thérèse being wounded "to the depths of her soul," and she titles this section of her study, "The Soul's Disillusionment." However, Thérèse herself flatly denies this in her autobiography. Writing about the happiness she experienced at finally entering Carmel, she said:

That happiness was not a passing kind which faded away with the "illusions of the first days." And speaking of illusions, the good God gave me the grace of not having any in entering Carmel. I found the religious life exactly what I had expected. None of the sacrifices surprised me, and yet you know, my dear mother, that my first days found more thorns than roses.

This passage was not written at the time of Thérèse's entrance into the convent, but near the end of her life. It is placed in an important position in her memoirs: at the very beginning of the section on her life in the convent where she recapitulates her whole impression of it. Goerres and Robo think that Thérèse was stunned at what she found in the Carmel, that she was bitterly disillusioned, that she had to rethink the whole religious life in terms of the unpleasant realities around her. All of that might make intriguing drama, but it does not square with what the saint affirmed. Thérèse said she had no illusions, no prior misconceptions, and she writes the phrase with striking vigor—almost, it might seem, in anticipatory rebuttal to her posthumous critics. She underlines the passage heavily beneath four of the words, and the word *aucune* (any; i.e., *any* illusions) is underlined twice. And here we reach that impasse again: the saint, writing as honestly and as objectively as she could, says she found no surprises in the religious life; the critics, writing forty to fifty years later, say she did.

St. Thérèse's reaction, her failure to be surprised by whatever peculiarity of personality she encountered, is important since it demonstrates her unfailing good sense and her mature acceptance of human nature.

4. THE INTERIOR CARMEL

The testimony at the trial reveals that some of the nuns thought Thérèse's life was rather tranquil, unmarred by any great suffering. This can only be a tribute to her control and self-mastery, since even a casual reading of her autobiography and letters demonstrates that she suffered quite a bit during the years she spent in the convent. There were the manifest trials like the severity of Mother Gonzague's treatment and the prolonged illness of her father,[1] but the most intense ones were those she suffered interiorly, unknown to anyone else. She wrote:

During the next five years, this way (of suffering) was mine. But there was no exterior manifestation of my suffering, and the fact that only I knew about it made it even more bitter. What surprises there will be at the end of life when we find out what really happened in some souls. Some people will be astonished at the way of suffering by which God led my soul.

Thérèse was being led through a way of aridity, a failure to receive any satisfaction or consolation in her prayers or religious duties. It is the most painful of all trials, one God uses to detach the soul from every human support so that it might be thrust entirely on Him. Apart from occasional, and often fleeting, periods of light and intense joy, Thérèse walked this path for almost the first six years of her religious life. She prayed without feeling, without emotion, but she continued to pray, to fulfill her religious duties, to refuse the good God nothing. "Dryness in prayer was my daily bread," she writes, "and even though I was deprived of all consolation, I was still the happiest of creatures because all my desires were fulfilled." And during her retreat before her profession of vows she wrote: ". . . it [the retreat] brought no consolation, only complete aridity and almost a sense of desolation."

Evaluating her life according to the principles of spiritual theology, we would call this "the dark night of the spirit," that period of more complete purification in which God leads the soul to an even closer union. During her seventeenth and eighteenth years, the works of St. John of the Cross were her only spiritual reading, and from them she undoubtedly learned what God was accomplishing in her soul: a new and deeper purge leading to unbelievable closeness with God.

Characteristic of this phase of the spiritual life, St. Thérèse notes that she maintained a constant and continual peace, despite her inability to receive any consolation in spiritual things. She writes: ". . . my soul rested in a sweet and profound peace which is almost impossible to explain; for seven and a half years now this intimate peace has been my portion, and it never left me even in the midst of my greatest trials." Thus, we see that strange, almost incomprehensible situation of the dark night of the spirit: on the one hand there is dryness, aridity, weariness; and yet on the other, there is a peace and gentle tranquility beneath it all—the peace of knowing that, despite the inability to see or taste, the soul is still loving God, and proving it in the most virile, most heroic manner.

Thérèse once discussed her aridity with Pauline, demonstrating a fine perception of what it meant:

My spouse says nothing to me, and I say nothing to Him, except that I love Him more than myself. I am happy to have no consolation. I would be ashamed if I were like those earthly lovers who are always looking at the hands of their spouse to see if he has brought a gift or watching his face for an entrancing smile.

To love, and yet to live without feeling the effects of love—that was Thérèse's lot during this period of her life.

5. THE WAY

Thérèse has captured the enthusiasm and admiration of the Popes, but there is no aspect of her life and doctrine which has fascinated them more than the "Little Way." Pope Benedict XV said that it contained "the secret of sanctity for all the faithful of the entire world." And Pope Pius XI stated: "If this way of spiritual childhood were practiced everywhere, it would bring about the reform of human society."

Intricate studies and ponderous volumes have been written explaining the Little Way, its significance, its meaning, its application. And yet the more it is explained, the more complicated it seems. In Thérèse's mind, and in the mind of the Popes, the Little Way was an eminently simple, eminently practical thing. There was nothing new about it—new, in the sense of an original discovery—but it was a fresh and vigorous restatement of basic Christian truths, long known but sometimes forgotten or minimized. Pius XI defined the Little Way by saying it "consists in feeling and acting under the discipline of virtue as a child feels and acts by nature." According to this definition, the Little Way is not a single virtue, nor less a facile device, but it is a whole attitude of soul, the basis of an entire relationship with God. It was the result of Thérèse's understanding of God—from the Scriptures, the teaching of the Church, and her own personal experience with Him.

About six weeks before her death, someone in the infirmary asked her to explain the Little Way; she said:

It is to recognize one's own nothingness, to expect everything from the good God as a child expects everything from its father. It is to be concerned about nothing, not even about making one's fortune. Even poor people give their children everything that is necessary for them; but as soon as a child grows up, his father will no longer support him but will say: "Go to work now, you can support yourself." *Eh bien,* it is because I never want to hear those words that I do not want to grow up—I am unable to earn my own living, the eternal life of heaven. Thus, I remain a child with no other occupation than gathering flowers, the flowers of love and sacrifice, and offering them to the good God for His pleasure. Being a child means not attributing to yourself the virtues you practice or believing yourself capable of anything at all; it means recognizing that the good God places the treasure of virtue in the hands of His child to be used when there is need of it —but it is still God's treasure. Finally, it means never being discouraged by your faults, because children fall frequently but are too small to hurt themselves much.

Beneath the fulsome phraseology, Thérèse's thought stands out, bright and challenging. She understands God; she treats Him as a father; she has complete trust and confidence in Him. It is this immediacy of contact with God, this fantastic confidence in Him, that forms the basis of the Little Way; it is, as Pius XI suggests, treating God just as a child treats his father. It is not assuming a coy posture before God (Pauline said that Thérèse only used the word "child" to better express her thought), but it is a vital awakening of one's faith, love, confidence, humility.

Thérèse, therefore, reintroduces us to God, our Father. She reminds us that we ourselves are nothing and He is everything. She shows us His goodness, and asks us to have unshakable confidence in Him. In a word, she places us squarely before God, with the proper dispositions and attitudes.

Thérèse's insistence on trust in God, even when we fail Him, is open to misinterpretations, and she once told Sister Marie of the Trinity to be careful how she explained it because it could possibly be taken for quietism, a heresy which counseled an indifference and unconcern about one's sins. "Do not believe that following the way of love is following a way of repose, full of sweetness and consolations," she said. "Quite to the contrary: it is to offer oneself as a victim for love, to give oneself without reserve to the divine pleasure, to partake with Jesus in His humiliations and His bitter chalice." And she told Céline:

One must do everything in his power, giving without counting the cost, renouncing oneself constantly, proving his love by all the deeds in our power. But even that is almost nothing. When we have done all we believe ourselves capable of, we must admit we are unprofitable servants, hoping that the good God by His grace will fulfill our desires. Little souls who run in the way of childhood hope for that. And I say "run," and not "rest."

Yet, Thérèse's audacious confidence in God and her astonishing intimacy with Him must not be attributed only to a personal condition of her own life, her constant innocence and freedom from serious sin. She wrote, in the last few lines of her autobiography: "I am certain that if my conscience were burdened with every possible sin, I would still cast myself into Jesus' arms, my heart bursting with repentance; for I know how He cherishes the prodigal child who returns to Him." Her Way is not a program merely for people fortunate enough to have lived in innocence; it is rather an invitation to all souls, the strong and the weak, the innocent and the repentant, to discover the reality and the mercy and the love of God.

There is excitement in Thérèse's words, the excitement of meeting God, of knowing Him as a person. And there is unspeakable peace, too, the peace of being able to cast off one's pretensions and approach God humbly, the peace of knowing He will take care of us. This is why Pope Benedict XV said: "There is a call to the faithful of every nation, no matter what be their age, sex or state of life, to enter wholeheartedly upon this way which led Sister Thérèse of the Child Jesus to the summit of heroic virtue."

6. THE NOVICE MISTRESS

When Pauline was elected prioress in 1893, Mother Gonzague was then made novice mistress. It was an office she held in name only, since Thérèse was appointed her assistant and actually had complete supervision of the novices. Pope Benedict XV said Thérèse was appointed novice mistress because of "the general esteem she enjoyed in the community," and she received the office "despite her youth and the short time since her profession."

The office required great tact on Thérèse's part because every so often Mother Gonzague would remember her title and begin to issue contradictory and confusing commands. Thérèse was equal to the situation, and by her prudence and her calmness she prevented the novitiate from being thrown into turmoil. Père Lemmonier, who preached the retreat at the convent for three consecutive years, said that the novices were completely satisfied with Thérèse; he stated at the trial that the novices considered her "very virtuous, very enlightened, and able to give extremely sound judgements about the spiritual life." Canon Peter Fauchon, the extraordinary confessor at the Carmel, offered the same kind of testimony: he said Thérèse "enlightened them, dispelled their doubts, consoled them, encouraged them, and seemed to be able to read their souls."

Thérèse's own novices who testified at the trial also were enthusiastic about her direction and government. Sister Marie of the Trinity, who had previously been in another Carmelite convent and was having a difficult time in the Lisieux Carmel, recorded her indebtedness to Thérèse: "She alone consoled me, encouraged me, and pleaded my cause with the other sisters." Thérèse once said to Marie of the Trinity: "How gladly would I give my very life so that you might be successful in your vocation." And the former novice recalled that when she finally made her profession of vows, Thérèse said it was among the most beautiful days in her own life.

Some of the novices were intractable and refractory, particularly Sister Martha of Jesus, the lay sister who was eight years Thérèse's senior. "I realize that I often exercised her virtue," Martha said, "and I am convinced that any other nun in her place would have abandoned me because I was so unbearable. But she always treated me with much love and charity, without showing the least annoyance." Martha herself related some of these episodes at the trial:

One day when I was feeling discouraged, I said something unkind to her, but she seemed not even to notice it and began talking to me kindly about some task we were doing together . . . Once I tried to test her virtue by seeing just how far her patience could be pushed. I refused to answer her when she asked me a question. However, I could not destroy her even temper, and ended up by asking her forgiveness . . . I have often wondered whatever could have interested her so much in a little lay sister. The great amount of zeal she had for my soul is beyond description.

But Thérèse could be firm, too, demanding a generosity from her novices. Her private conferences with them were frank and honest discussions. She had a passion for truth, and Sister Marie of the Trinity recalls her saying: "I owe you the truth. Dislike me for it, if you want, but I will tell you the truth right up until my death." To one novice who had made her bed badly, Thérèse said: "Is that how you would have made the bed of the Infant Jesus? Why have you come to Carmel if you are not going to lead a spiritual life? It would be better if you stayed in the world and did some useful and external things." When a nun was slowly walking her morning assignment, Thérèse approached her—"Is that the way people in the world go to work when they have children and must work to support them?"

This firm side of Thérèse's character has prompted

some biographers to see her as the legendary French religious superior of the last century: rigid, unbending, highly critical, and arrogantly aggressive. Ironically, the Devil's Advocate accused her of being a *poor* superior because she did not correct the novices enough. "A superior does not do his duty if he fails to stamp out abuses, repress the insolent, and safeguard his own authority and common discipline," the Devil's Advocate said. Reference was made especially to some of Pauline's testimony about Thérèse:

> She allowed the novices to voice whatever complaint they had about her. They felt more free with her because she was not the real novice mistress and was younger than many of them. I remember one day when a novice spoke to her in a rather humiliating way. She had a joyful expression on her face, and I said to her: "Are you all right?" She answered: "I am very happy. The good God gave me the opportunity of learning how very little I am and how very little virtue I possess. I thought of Semei cursing David, and I said to myself, 'Yes, it is the Lord who ordered that Sister to say those things to me.' What made me even more convinced of it was that this morning I had an intense desire to be humiliated."

However, the response in the *Processus* commends Thérèse for her humility and prudence, noting that it was wise of her to allow the novices to talk their problems out, even when it was unflattering to her. Thérèse's mature and modern views on a religious superior's function are astonishing for one of her age and background. She understood that the competent religious superior cannot be imperious or autocratic, but must treat the members of a community with patience, kindness, understanding—

and this demands both humility and prudence, qualities she so clearly possessed. The novices must have been somewhat surprised at Thérèse's deportment as superior. Far from expecting a gentle superior, they had every right to expect a rigid one: she was only twenty years of age, and young people in positions of authority tend to be idealistic and unyielding; and her absolute and continual fidelity to the rule could only make them feel she would be as hard on them as she was on herself. Her resiliency and her patience must have both astonished and delighted the novices in the Lisieux Carmel.

Sister Marie of the Trinity testified about one incident of spiritual direction in which Thérèse demonstrated her realistic view of life. Sister Marie said she had been having problems understanding the virtue of chastity, and the confessor, Abbé Jouf, could not spare time in the confessional to discuss the matter with her. She was afraid of Mother Gonzague, thus she timorously approached Thérèse. "I am afraid you will not understand anything about the troubles in my soul," she told Thérèse. (Céline reported elsewhere in the testimony that Thérèse confided to her that she had never suffered any temptation against chastity in her whole life.) The young novice mistress smiled and said: "Do you believe that purity consists in ignorance of evil? You can confide in me anything you want without any fear; nothing astonishes me." And Sister Marie notes that Thérèse deftly dispelled her problem by distinguishing between temptation and consent.

Pauline, during a conversation in the convent one day, discovered that her younger sister was acquainted with what she euphemistically called "the facts of life" (*des choses de la vie*) and asked where she had received instruction:

She answered she had discovered these things quite by accident while observing flowers and birds. Then she added: "But the Blessed Virgin knew all that. On Annunciation Day did she not say to the angel, "How shall this be for I know not man?" Knowledge of these things is not bad. The good God has made all things good and noble. Marriage is good for those who are called to that state; only sin disfigures and sullies it."

This wholesome attitude is far removed from the puritanism and unhealthy disdain of life that Thérèse's modern critics see in her. One incident from her life is used, with depressing monotony, to "prove" her puritanical attitude: the episode when Céline, still a young lay woman, visited her sister in the convent parlor, and Thérèse tried to dissuade her from attending a dance. She pleaded with her, reasoned with her, and finally wept—in fact, "she wept as she had never wept before." Nevertheless, Céline attended the dance, but when a young man took her out on the dance floor they found themselves, inexplicably, unable to coordinate their movements and finally retired from the floor in acute embarrassment. Céline attributed her sudden and strange clumsiness to Thérèse's prayers. Commenting on the episode, Robo states that Thérèse treated her sister "with a puritanical severity that to us sounds greatly exaggerated" (p. 111). And so it might seem—except that one important bit of evidence is not cited. Céline, even before her entrance into the convent, had taken a perpetual vow of chastity, a special vow to avoid sins of impurity and even refrain from marriage. Very few directors or confessors would allow a person with a perpetual vow of chastity to go dancing or on dates; one might dispute the wisdom of taking this vow in a particular case, but one cannot dispute its obligations. Seen in this light, Thérèse's insistence that her sister, bound by a vow of chastity, refrain from dancing does not seem so ill-advised or puritanical.

Although Thérèse was able to give sound advice and direction to her novices, she herself had very little protracted direction from priests throughout her life. "Jesus alone is my guide," she wrote. She has been criticized for her attitude in this regard. Father Robo says she has "a doctrine which, taken too literally, might authorize Protestants to claim St. Teresa as a champion of private judgement . . ."; and he claims, "Her statements may appear sometimes a bit unguarded" (p. 128). The Devil's Advocate for her cause made similar charges, stating: "She seldom followed the advice of directors or their authority, considering instead her own private thoughts as divine lights." The response, of course, rejects the charge. Père Pichon, her Jesuit confessor, testified about the direction he gave her:

From the time I first knew her, that is from the age of seven, the Servant of God confided in me about her desire to consecrate herself to God. As far as her precise desire to become a Carmelite, I am not quite sure whether she spoke to me about that before or after her sister, Pauline, entered the convent.

Then the judges asked him if she followed his advice, and he answered:

I can affirm that she took counsel. She consulted me about her spiritual life, and particularly about her vocation. She did not pour herself out in a flurry of words. She asked her questions very simply, but with an intense seriousness, without insisting on her own opinion.

Père Pichon was reassigned to Canada shortly after her entrance into Carmel, and she never saw him again. Thus, she lost the only real director she ever had. But during the rest of her life, she continually consulted the priests who came to the convent for retreats or confession—Lemmonier, Blinot, Jouf, Prou, Madelaine, to name a few. (She, incidentally, did not always receive the most sage advice from these men: Père Blinot told her that her aspirations to be a saint were presumptuous; and the priest who heard her confession during her temptations against faith in the last months of her life told her severely that her soul was in a dangerous state.) It was Père Alexis Prou who confirmed her doctrine of the Little Way, and Père Lemmonier studied her act of oblation, making some corrections in it. Many of these priests testified at the trial, relating detailed accounts of the state of her soul, and Msgr. Toeschi's response to the Devil's Advocate says: "If the confessors and directors of her soul knew her so well, it could only have been because she had opened her soul to them." The response also praised Thérèse for having Jesus as her only director, interpreting this as fidelity to actual grace, that impulse of the Spirit within, prompting and inspiring us when we cannot approach a director, even if we have one.

Two arresting facts should be noted, though. First, Thérèse had difficulty in communicating, in pouring out her inmost thoughts to a priest. She admitted the same problem with Mother Marie of the Angels, her novice mistress, a holy soul, but one with whom she was unable to communicate on that intimate level. Only rarely did she find a priest with whom she could really feel at ease—Pichon was certainly one, and Godfrey Madelaine appears to have been another. Secondly, during the last nine years of her life, the only adult years she knew, she had no real director, only priests who gave her advice in confession.

But is not Pope Pius' statement—"without going beyond the common order of things"—verified even here? How few of us really feel at ease in discussing our most personal affairs with a priest? And even if we want to, how few of us can find a priest in whom we can confide, or who can give us the necessary time? Much is written about the necessity of a spiritual director, and certainly no one will deny it, but in the practical realm how many people actually enjoy the benefit of a true spiritual director? St. Teresa of Avila could not find a competent spiritual director until she was forty years old. And Thérèse did not have one for the whole last period of her life. Even in this she is like us.

CHAPTER VI

CONSUMMATION

1. THE SUMMIT

Dom Godfrey Madelaine, who knew Thérèse well, said that her autobiography contains an evident account of her "constant and amazing progression in the sublimity of her virtues and in the development of her doctrine." Progression and development, then, are the key factors explaining her spiritual journey. It was a progression stimulated by prayer, even when her prayer was clouded with aridities; by mortification, which consisted in accepting the sufferings God sent her, and in undertaking a program of hidden, almost microscopic acts of self-denial; by fidelity to grace, following the quiet inspiration of the Spirit, directing her, illuminating her, guiding her.

The fruition of this program came in 1895. While attending the community Mass on the ninth of June, the feast of the Blessed Trinity, she felt a compelling desire to offer herself as a complete victim to the Merciful Love of God. She writes about it in her autobiography:

This year on the ninth of June, the feast of the Blessed Trinity, I received the grace of understanding more

than ever before how much Jesus wants to be loved. I
was thinking about souls who offer themselves as victims to the Divine Justice for the purpose of taking upon
themselves the punishments which sinners deserve . . .
I cried from the depths of my heart: My God, why is it
only Your Justice which receives souls who offer themselves as victims? Should there not be victims to Your
Merciful Love as well? . . . O my Jesus, grant me the
happiness of becoming such a victim; consume Your
holocaust through the fire of Your Divine Love.

She discussed her plan with the prioress, Pauline, and
received her permission to compose a formula of oblation.
On Tuesday, the eleventh, she recited her act of oblation
in the chapel. The oblation is a moving document of total
surrender, a statement of her desire to become a victim of
expiation for sinners. Its basic tone is one of vibrant love,
beginning with the opening phrase, "O my God, O Most
Blessed Trinity, I want to love You and make You loved,"
down to the concluding sentence, "O my Beloved, I desire
to renew this oblation with every beat of my heart, an infinite number of times, until the shadows fade away and
I can forever tell You my love face to face."

On Friday of that same week, the fourteenth of June,
she was making the stations of the cross by herself in the
chapel when she experienced her "wound of love."

I had just begun the Stations of the Cross in choir when
all at once I felt myself wounded by a shaft of fire (*d'un
trait de feu*) so strong that I thought it would kill me.
I do not know how to explain it; it was as if some
invisible hand had immersed me in a fire. O what fire
and sweetness at the same time! I was burning with fire
and I thought that one minute, even one second, more

its intensity would kill me. I then understood the statements of the saints about these states which they so often experienced.

From this moment on, she moved into a new level of spiritual existence, a state in which she was inundated with God's love. "Ah, since that day," she wrote, "it seems that Love penetrates me and surrounds me; it seems that at each moment this Merciful Love renews me, purifies my soul, and allows no trace of sin in it."

Even her writing, her very style, becomes more lyrical and more intense, as she writes:

I do not desire either suffering or death, although both are appealing to me; it is love alone which really attracts me . . . I can ask for nothing with any enthusiasm except the perfect accomplishment of the Divine Will in my soul, unhindered by any intrusion of created things. I can say, with the words of our father, St. John of the Cross, in his *Spiritual Canticle,* "I drank in the inner cellar of my Beloved, and when I went forth into the meadow I forgot everything and lost the flock which I used to drive. My soul has employed all its resources in His service; now I guard no flock, nor do I have any other duties. Now my only occupation is love." Or again: "I know love is so powerful that it can turn whatever is good or bad in me into profit, and it can transform my soul into Himself."

Undoubtedly, Thérèse was living in what theologians call the "spiritual espousals," a state of transforming union in which the soul achieves a complete union with God, becoming entranced with Him, thinking with Him, acting with Him. Her actions and sentiments during this period offer adequate proof of this, but even stronger proof is furnished by Thérèse herself in the passage cited immediately above. She is quoting from St. John of the Cross, using his doctrine to describe her own spiritual state. And St. John is describing a soul in the state of transforming union![1] Thérèse was well acquainted with the writings of this Doctor of the Church—she read nothing else for two whole years—and when she points out her own spiritual position in his writings, we can only presume she knows what she is doing.

Her mystical wounding by God's love bears a marked similarity to the transverberation of St. Teresa of Avila—an episode which is commemorated in the Carmelite Order by a special Mass and Office on August 27. We have few details about Thérèse's wounding apart from her statement quoted above. We do, however, find a fuller explanation and corroboration of this phenomenon in the writings of St. John of the Cross. He says: "When the soul is enkindled in the love of God . . . it will be conscious of an assault upon it made by a seraph with an arrow or a dart burning with a fire of love, which will pierce the soul, now enkindled like a coal, or to speak more truly, like a flame, and will cauterize it in the most sublime manner."[2] St. John contends that this wounding is not a physical phenomenon, but a spiritual action of God which strongly resembles a burn suffered by fire; the ultimate purpose of the phenomenon is an immense intensification of love in the soul—all of which seems to be verified in Thérèse's case.

There is no other episode similar to this in Thérèse's life, although Pauline testified she did experience a profound contemplative prayer on a number of occasions. Thérèse told her that even before her entrance into the convent she had many "transports of love," and during her novitiate she had a religious experience that lasted for eight days:

It was as if a veil had been thrown over me hiding all
created things. I seemed to be completely hidden beneath the veil of the Blessed Virgin. I had charge of
the refectory, and I did my work as if I were in a dream,
as though I were living in a borrowed body. I remained
in that state for an entire week. It was a supernatural
state, very difficult to explain.

Thérèse also told Pauline:

A number of times in the cloister garden during the
time of the great silence, I felt myself to be in such a
profound recollection and my heart so united to the
good God that I effortlessly made extremely ardent acts
of love. It definitely seems to me that these graces were
"flights of the spirit," as St. Teresa calls them.

But none of these manifestations of her sanctity
equalled the episode of her "wound of love." She admitted to Pauline: "From the age of fourteen I experienced
assaults of love. And how much I loved God during them!
But those cannot be compared to what happened after
I made my Offering to Love. Only then did I feel myself
being burned by an intense flame."

Even her practice of fraternal charity developed as she
comprehended new refinements of that virtue. "During
this past year, my dear mother, the good God gave me the
grace of understanding what charity is; of course, I
understood it before, but only in a rather imperfect way,"
she wrote. Her kindness, her patience, her tolerance toward the nuns in the community had been part of her
program to love God, to see God in their souls. But her
new and deeper union with God made her aware of something else. She quotes the statement of Christ at the Last
Supper: "A new commandment I give you, that you love

one another; that as I have loved you, you also love one another," and she concludes we are to love people *as Jesus* loves them, with the same kind of love He bore for them. It is one thing to be kind to people because we respect and love the God dwelling within them, but it is a more profound and more penetrating thing to love these people just as God does, regarding them from God's viewpoint, acting toward them as God does. This demands a close union with God, attempting to adopt His thoughts and His love for people, not being limited to one's own personal considerations, or even one's own minor heroisms in dealing with people. "When I am charitable, I feel it is Jesus Himself who is acting in me," she writes, "and the more united I am to Him, the more I love each one of my sisters." Her union with God was productive of an even greater sympathy for people, because she was able to adopt God's own thoughts about them—it was "Jesus Himself who is acting in me."

In June of 1895, therefore, Thérèse had reached full union with God, the summit of the spiritual life. She was twenty-two years old, and the purifying nights of sense and spirit were behind her. Now her only concern was, as she said, "to love Jesus even unto folly."

2. THE FINAL GIFT

On the evening of April 2, 1896, Thérèse suffered her first hemorrhage, a flush of blood rushing to her mouth. She had just laid her head on the pillow when this preliminary attack occurred, but she remained in bed, waiting until morning to investigate the full extent of the attack. She reported it to her superior but protested that she felt well enough to continue the monastic penances of Holy Week. A whole year elapsed before her illness reached the critical stage, and during that year she followed the full monastic regime, but at the cost of great physical effort. She received a series of treatments from the convent doctor, who at first felt her illness was slight and passing. Even the nuns shared that opinion for a while, an opinion undoubtedly strengthened by the vigor with which Thérèse was able to follow the monastic observance, and by the healthy-looking flush in her cheeks, that deceiving phenomenon which occurs in the early stages of tuberculosis.

But her greatest problems during the last eighteen months of her life were spiritual and not physical. On Easter Sunday, 1896, two days after the first hemorrhage, she was plunged into her trial of faith. She describes it in her autobiography:

> During those happy days of Eastertime, Jesus taught me that there are souls who do not have faith, and through the abuse of grace they lose that treasure which is the source of all true and pure happiness. He allowed my soul to be cast into impenetrable darkness, and the thought of heaven, ordinarily so sweet for me, became a subject of conflict and torment. This trial did not last for days, or even weeks; it was to last until the hour God decided it should stop, and that hour has not yet arrived. I wish I could explain to you what I am going through, but I believe it is impossible: you would have to pass through this dark tunnel to understand the obscurity.

These temptations against faith lasted up until Thérèse's death, and they constituted the most severe trial of her life. She was continually battling against unwanted thoughts which protested the reality of a future life. There seemed to be no one particular tenet of the faith which troubled her; it was simply that the whole supernatural world became suddenly unreal, and she had to make constant acts of faith to reassert her belief. As a tangible act of her basic position, she obtained permission from her confessor to write the Creed in her own blood, and she inscribed it in the blank pages in the back of the small Gospel book she carried over her heart—this book is still preserved at the Carmel, the words of the Creed now somewhat faded and a dark brown. Dom Godfrey Madelaine advised her during this period, and at the trial he commented on the serenity with which she endured this ordeal and the unconquerable faith by which she was able to deny these grim thoughts.

But an important question asserts itself: what was her spiritual position at that time? If she had passed through the dark nights, why was she compelled to undergo another period of suffering? According to the doctrine of St. John of the Cross, the soul in the state of perfect union will still experience sufferings, indeed more grievous sufferings than anything yet endured in the process of spiritual growth. But the sufferings of the night are purifying and purgative trials geared to detaching the soul from self-love and projecting it into union with God; while the sufferings of the purified soul are redemptive trials for the good of souls and the Church. These trials accomplish a union and identification with the Crucified Christ. Thus, St. John of the Cross writes of the soul in union with God: ". . . it would be a great consolation and joy for her to pass through all the afflictions and trials of the world . . . suffering is most delectable and profitable to her . . . the purest suffering brings with it the most intimate and purest knowledge."[3]

Thérèse herself regarded the temptations against faith as redemptive, something offered to God as reparation for sinners and unbelievers. She writes about her ordeal:

My Lord, your child has understood your divine light and asks pardon for her brothers; she is willing to eat the bread of sadness as long as you want her to, and she will not rise from this bitter table where sinners eat until you indicate it. Meanwhile, she can only say in her name and in the name of her brothers: "Have mercy on us, Lord, for we are all poor sinners."

I say to Jesus that I am happy not enjoying the sight of that beautiful heaven here on earth, as long as He opens it in eternity for unbelievers.

If, through some impossibility, you did not see my suffering, I would still be happy to suffer if by it I could hinder or offer reparation for some fault against the faith.

This was Thérèse's own evaluation of her temptations against faith, and it seems also to be the evaluation of Pope Pius XII. In his radio address of 1954, he spoke of her "extreme agony in pure faith with all consolation gone," and said: "But St. Thérèse knows she is presenting an expiatory offering for the sins of the world, that she is continuing in her lacerated flesh and heart the mystery of the Cross."[4]

During this last trial of her life, however, she maintained a basic peace and serenity in her soul, just as she had in her earlier interior trials. The lyrical tone of her writings continued; in fact, the section of the autobiography addressed to Marie, which was written at the actual time of her temptations, contains the most intense sentiments of love in the entire manuscript.

O, Jesus, my beloved, how can I explain with what tenderness and sweetness you are leading my soul, and how you send the light of your grace through the middle of the storm raging around me.

I cannot imagine what I will possess after my death that I do not possess now. It is true, I will see the good God; but as for being with Him, I already have that here on earth.

Thus, the light and the love endured through the storm. Pauline adds a curious and intriguing footnote to Thérèse's attitude during the ordeal of faith; she asked her sister one day: "Is the Blessed Virgin also hidden from you?" "No," Thérèse answered, "the Blessed Virgin is never hidden from me. And when I can no longer see the good God, she takes care of all my dealings with Him. I commission her especially to tell Him to have no fear of sending me trials."

3. "MY GOD, I LOVE YOU"

Thérèse tried to continue the monastic observance as long as she could, but her tubercular condition was enervating her more and more. The simplest activities began to require immense effort. When she climbed the single flight of stairs to her cell, she had to stop on every step and regain her breath. It sometimes took her a full hour to undress. Finally, on the evening of July 8, 1897, she was placed in the convent infirmary on the first floor. But even then she tried to force herself into doing as much as she could. One of the nuns was guiding her on a walk in the garden when she decided Thérèse was fatiguing herself; but Thérèse insisted they continue because, as she said, she was taking those painful and tiring steps for some missionary in a distant land.

Some of the biographers maintain that she received inadequate care during her final illness. It is a matter of record that she received little treatment during the first months after her initial hemorrhage, but she demanded little and Dr. de Cornieres had pronounced her illness to be a minor ailment. But when the full extent of her sickness was realized it seemed that Mother Gonzague was extremely generous in taking care of the sick nun. Thérèse wrote to the prioress that she was becoming embarrassed by the variety of medicines purchased for her: ". . . no medicine seems to be too expensive; if one fails you try another." Her sentiments of gratitude for Mother Gonzague's charity are apparently genuine and represent a report on the true situation. There was only one medicine the prioress refused to purchase: morphine. But this was a product of her own rigorous conviction that Carmelite nuns should not be drugged. We can rightfully disagree with this strange and peculiar conviction, but we can hardly accuse the prioress of indifference toward the sick, or even worse, of a persecution against Thérèse. Mother Gonzague also permitted Thérèse's sisters to spend long hours with her each day in the infirmary, and she appointed Céline to be her special infirmarian, allowing her to live in the small room adjoining the infirmary.

There is one episode, however, which is more difficult to evaluate in the light of Mother Gonzague's other kindnesses to Thérèse. When the convent doctor, Dr. de Cornieres, took a month's vacation in August, his patients were placed under the care of Dr. La Néele. The young doctor said he felt Thérèse should be visited every day, but Mother Gonzague only allowed him in the cloister three times during that period. Perhaps the prioress had no confidence in the substitute doctor's opinion? Perhaps she felt it was too late now since Thérèse had already been anointed? Or perhaps the evaluation of some critics is correct—that the prioress was afraid of Dr. La Néele's

influence in the convent? Dr. La Néele had married Thérèse's cousin, Jeanne Guérin, and was, therefore, a relative
by marriage to the Martin sisters; it is thus conceivable
that, given Mother Gonzague's personality, she could have
feared the presence behind the cloister walls of a male
and authoritative person who might lend dignity to the opposing faction. We shall never know with any certainty.

At any rate, Thérèse's illness was beyond the help of
any physician—or of any medical procedures of the time.
The doctor and the nuns who attended her all testified to
her serenity and calmness in the face of the excruciating
pains she was undergoing. Propped up in her bed, she
smiled, she dispensed kindnesses, but most of all she suffered. The Decree of Beatification speaks of her terrible
sickness and her almost five months in bed, and it states:
"She endured severe sufferings with a cheerful face and
amazing patience."

During those five months, Pauline took notes of any
inspiring and informative statement made by Thérèse,
and she also prodded her sister into answering questions
about her religious perceptions, all duly recorded. These
notes have since been published as the book *Novissima
Verba* (Latin for the rather unimaginative title, "Last
Words"). Reading the book, one might feel that the questions posed to the dying nun are importunate and clumsy,
that they needlessly fatigued her. She was asked when
she wanted God to take her; how it was she lived without
fear; how she would spend her life if she had it all to do
over again; what the Little Way meant—and a host of
similar insistent questions. Thérèse answered them all
with patience and kindness, and her recorded statements
of the last five months of her life serve as a splendid re-
capitulation of her doctine. But one gets the impression
that she was somewhat amused by the sisters hovering
around her, artlessly prying statements out of her. They

told her about a dying priest who refused the least alle-
viation in his final illness, and she shrugged her shoulders,
saying, "In my Father's house there are many mansions."
She was asked what she would die of, and she answered
wryly: "I will die of death." (The gentle irony seems to
have been lost on Pauline.) On one occasion, Pauline
tried to induce her to say "some words of edification to
the doctor," but Thérèse refused. "Oh, *ma mère*, that's
not my way of doing things. Let the doctor think whatever he wants. I love only simplicity and have a horror of
the contrary. I assure you that to do as you want would
be very wrong of me."

Her unusual self-control, therefore, was in evidence until the end of her life. She was wasting away from the
painful tubercular condition, but she retained her self-
mastery, her complete command of herself. Some unpleasant medicine was given her, and she insisted on drinking
it slowly as a mortification, rather than forcing it down
quickly. We noted how distressed she was when someone
gave her a doll for her diversion, and we see above her
refusal to allow Pauline to take command of her thinking.
Father Robo's suggestion that Thérèse fell under the spell
of Pauline and became a mere mouthpiece for her older
sister (cf. pp. 186–187) is simply not supported by the
facts.

Sometime in June or July of 1897, a surprising development took place: Thérèse, who had lived such a hidden
and retired existence (the Bull of Canonization says:
"She imitated the hidden life of the Virgin Mary in Naz-
areth"), now became suddenly convinced that a world-
wide mission was soon to begin for her after she died. "I
feel my mission is about to begin, my mission of making
souls love God as I love Him, my mission of teaching my

little way to souls. If my desires are fulfilled, I shall
spend my heaven upon earth until the end of the world.
Yes, I shall spend my heaven in doing good upon earth."
As the weeks and months passed, her statements became
more firm, more absolute. "I know the whole world will
love me." "I will send down a shower of roses." "Will you
look down?" she was asked. "No, I will come down."

She told Marie about the projects she would do in
heaven. "What projects?" Marie asked. "I will begin my
mission. I will come down to aid missionaries and to obtain the baptism of pagan children before they die." Pauline told her they would put a palm branch in her hand
after her death. "Yes," Thérèse said, "but I will have to
let it slip from my hands because I will use them to
shower graces."

In the middle of August, she suddenly said to her sisters: "You know very well you are taking care of a saint,
don't you?" She permitted her personal articles to be kept
as use for future relics, and she even told her sisters to
gather up some rose petals she had been holding so that
they might be distributed to people later.

And the manuscript she had written—the personal,
rambling memoirs intended for the nuns in the convent—
now became important in her mind. She told Pauline to
have it published as a book after her death, and gave her
full liberty to do any editing she felt necessary; but, she
insisted, it must be published without delay. She spoke of
the immense good the autobiography would accomplish.
She predicted that Pauline would not have time for grief
after her death because, "Until the end of her life she will
be so busy on my account that she will not have time to
suffer."

Something unusual had undoubtedly happened to
Thérèse. Ordinarily humble and self-effacing, she now
speaks openly of her own sanctity, her mission, her future

glorification. The dying nun who says, "The whole world will love me," does not sound like the humble nun who wrote, "O, Jesus, grant that nobody be concerned about me at all, that I may be forgotten, trodden under foot like a grain of sand." Was she stumbling blindly in the dark, making wild and brave predictions? Ida Goerres thinks so: "But we are inclined to see Thérèse's numerous conversations and promises of future deeds as a reaction against her temptations, as exercises in blind hope" (p. 381). However, Goerres' evaluation—which stands in opposition to that of the ecclesiastical judges and Pope Benedict XV—does not touch the real problem, the problem which was discussed in the process of canonization. The Devil's Advocate accused Thérèse of excessive confidence, indeed, of presumption, since "no one while he lives knows whether he is worthy of love or hate"; and he adds that the saints often passed their final days with great concern for their own salvation. Msgr. Toeschi's response studies the charge carefully, admitting that "if this objection stands, it is an insurmountable obstacle for the cause, one which would immediately bring about its defeat." The response then gives its answer: Thérèse was led by a "supernatural light," and she made those statements "not by her own reasoning, but under the inspiration of the Spirit of God!" The dialogue between the Devil's Advocate and the official response, therefore, places the problem in its proper perspective: either Thérèse was being directed by some kind of inspiration from God, or she was guilty of the sin of presumption and thus unworthy of canonization. There is no other alternative.

The more we think of the actual situation at the time of Thérèse's death, the more outrageous do her predictions become. Here is a sweet and pretty girl from the provinces, a cloistered nun for nine years, known only to a

handful of people in Normandy, the author of some uneventful childhood reminiscences hurriedly jotted down
in a child's notebook, distinguished for no accomplishment of any external significance—and yet she calmly says
she will be loved by the whole world and her simple reminiscences will become famous. She must be a frightfully
deluded person; or she must be specially inspired by
God.

In proving that Thérèse's prophesies were valid ones,
the response to the Devil's Advocate states the qualifi-
cations for a true prophecy, among which are two principal conditions—that the matter be clearly stated before
the event, and that the object of the prophecy be something which could not be caused by any natural agent.
Thérèse, of course, stated her prophecy in the most clear
and unequivocal manner; and the things she prophesied
—for example, the shower of roses, the miracles—were certainly beyond her own natural resources, or even those of
her sisters. "The proof from the results is the best proof,"
the response says, quoting an old Latin axiom. And the
results in this case provide an incontestable proof. The
things she predicted did happen, the shower of roses did
occur, the book was immensely popular, the whole world
did love her. Almost unbelievably, the dying consumptive nun was right. The *Processus* quotes the French theologian, Père Auriault: "Since the later events confirm the
prophecy, it is quite evident that God was preparing the
young virgin for a major work."

The judges also claim there is no opposition between a
person's individual humility and a revelation of future
glory. They quote the famous thesis of Pope Benedict
XIV, which cites a number of cases where saints predicted their canonizations and allowed relics to be preserved even before their deaths. St. Benedict Joseph Labre

predicted people would one day venerate his body; and the Capuchin, St. Felix of Cantalice, told his confreres that his garments would someday become precious and they would be envied for possessing them.

God, Who had led Thérèse along the rugged path to a close union with Him, was now revealing in her soul the vision of her future mission. Pope Benedict XV, in his address on the occasion of the *Super Dubio* decree, summarizes it in this manner: "She, who had been so humble throughout her life, could not at that final moment utter statements apparently in contradiction to humility unless she was acting directly under divine inspiration."

Thérèse's candid assertions of her future glory call attention to a germane subject: the ease with which she was able to discuss her own virtues and ultimate glorification. Some biographers find this rather disconcerting and feel she was unduly fascinated with herself. Robo said, "She always had a great opinion of her own importance," and he speaks of her "constant unconscious preoccupation with herself" (pp. 72–73). Goerres writes of "her own overstimulated awareness of herself" (p. 410), and states that her sisters "almost forced Thérèse to have too high an opinion of herself" (p. 403). These statements reveal a misunderstanding of the virtue of humility. The humble person is not unaware of the gifts, even the virtues, he possesses; he recognizes their presence, *but* he also recognizes the ultimate source of them, God. Humility is not a pose or a posture which artificially denies the real situation; it is, however, a penetrating insight which comprehends the real situation in all its ramifications. St. Teresa of Avila was able to define humility by the single word "truth"— the truth which realistically evaluates a person's worth, but just as realistically attributes it all to God. Thérèse, therefore, was certainly aware of the virtues she possessed

—we would think her an exceptionally slow and unperceptive person if she were not—but she was vitally conscious that it was all God's work. When Pauline was discussing the publication of the autobiography shortly before her death, Thérèse suddenly said: "But everyone will be able to recognize that all comes from God and that whatever glory I may have will be a free gift which is none of my doing." And she wrote to one of the missionary priests with whom she corresponded: "Do not think that humility consists in failing to recognize the gifts of the good God. I know that He has done great things in me, and every day I praise Him for it with a full heart."

We know that she was very much aware of her own inherent weakness, and the recognition of this weakness is one of the fundamentals of her Little Way. Her childhood confessor told her she was sinless, but without God's grace she would become a "little devil"; she accepted his statement implicitly, and it remained deeply ingrained in her throughout her life. She confesses herself to be "weak and imperfect," and she writes, "O my God, I am happy to feel myself little and weak in Your presence." Again: "The very greatest thing God has done for me is to have shown me my littleness, my basic incapacity for doing good." And even during her final illness in the infirmary: "How happy I am to feel so imperfect and so much in need of God's mercy at the moment of death!" Dom Godfrey Madelaine testified at the trial: "During my conversations with her, I discovered that she was an exceptionally honest and humble person. In my whole ministry, I do not believe I have ever found such a generous and humble soul."

But she could not deny the fact that God had preserved her from sin and was preparing her for an astonishing mission after her death. That would have been a falsification of fact. A statement she made while in the infirmary shows her personal resolution of the issue: "The good God shows me the truth. I understand quite well that all these gifts come from Him. Yes, it seems to me that I am being humble in proclaiming His mercies."

The witnesses at the trial referred to the *Magnificat*, the prayer of the Blessed Virgin, and in that prayer we discover the most profound explanation of this facet of Thérèse's life. The Blessed Virgin said:

> My soul magnifies the Lord,
>   and my spirit rejoices in God my Savior;
> Because He has regarded the lowliness of
>   His handmaid;
> For, behold, henceforth all generations
>   shall call me blessed;
> Because He who is mighty has done great things
>   for me, and holy is His name.[5]

The Blessed Virgin recognizes her position: all generations shall call her blessed; and He has done great things for her. But she also recognizes her personal relationship to God in it all: He has regarded the lowliness of His handmaid; and He who is mighty has done the great things. There is a striking similarity here even to the very phrases Thérèse uses. She, too, understood that "He has done great things in me," but she immediately attributes it all to the mercy of God. *He who is mighty* has done them. And holy is His name.

Thérèse's September days in the infirmary were racked with pain. Her breath came in short wheezes, and she was casting up phlegm continually. Sleep was almost an impossibility. "I did not think it was possible to suffer so

much," she said. A number of years before, she had cho-
sen the title "the Holy Face" as an addition to her reli-
gious name, and the full significance of the Savior's blood-
splattered countenance bore in upon her now. She was
Thérèse of the Child Jesus, but also Thérèse of the Holy
Face. Her Little Way included both the serenity of the
Child Jesus in Bethlehem and the agony of the crucified
Lord on Golgotha.

Shortly after seven o'clock on the evening of September
30, her breath grew fainter and more rapid. Then, dis-
tinctly and loudly, she said, "O I love Him!" She was gazing at her crucifix. Finally, after a few seconds: "My God,
I love You." Those were her last words.

Suddenly her eyes became transfixed, as if she were viewing something unseen by the nuns kneeling around the bed.
Pauline testified: "Her eyes . . . were full of life and fire
and joy . . . She was in ecstasy, having a vision . . ."
Sister Marie of the Angels said: "Her eyes, now shining
and magnificent, gazed at the statue of the Blessed Virgin,
as if she were seeing something supernatural." Sister
Thérèse of St. Augustine stated: "With no fear of exaggeration, I can say that an ecstasy transfigured her features for about the space of a *Credo*. The expression on
her face was so moving, I lowered my eyes." The Bull of
Canonization states that she died "consumed in an
ecstasy," and the Apostolic Brief for her beatification says
"she was given a heavenly vision."

Then she closed her eyes and died.

A few blocks up the street, Abbé Jouf was sick in bed.
He had been informed of Thérèse's illness and knew her
death was imminent. When he heard the convent bell
tolling the measured rhythm for a deceased soul, he
stared sadly out the window. "What a loss for Carmel,"
he said. "She is a saint." Some time previously he had

told Pauline: "She is an elite soul who grows from virtue to virtue. If she were only known, she would be the glory of Carmel."

Abbé Jouf could not have realized that God had plans for making her known.

CHAPTER VII

PROPAGANDA

1. THE MEMOIRS OF A SAINT

St. Thérèse's autobiography has become a phenomenal best seller, and yet it had the most improbable of beginnings. Up until the final months of her life, Thérèse had no suspicion or intention that her writings would ever be published. In fact, her autobiography was not composed as an integral book, but rather as three separate manuscripts later joined into one.

In January of 1895, Thérèse was entertaining the nuns one evening at the community recreation with some reminiscences of her childhood. Her sister Marie suddenly conceived the idea that Thérèse's recollections should be recorded as a family souvenir. M. Martin had died just six months previously, and Marie perhaps had been thinking about the now final dissolution of their family life at home. She presented her idea to Pauline, who was then prioress, while Thérèse smiled amusedly. But when Pauline agreed to the proposal, Thérèse's reaction was one of mild horror. "What do you want me to write about that you don't already know?" she asked. However, she complied with the prioress' order, although her misgivings about wasted time and useless effort continued for a while. She expresses these in the opening section of the manuscript addressed to Pauline: "That day when you asked me to do it, I was afraid my heart would become dissipated by introspection, but since then Jesus helped me to understand that I am pleasing Him by simple obedience." Significantly, she wrote the words "Notebook of obedience" on the jacket of the copy book she used for the task.

She was only able to donate odd moments of free time to her writing, and most of those were at night during the time of the solemn monastic silence in her cell. She used a portable wooden bench which she held propped on her knees, and her only light was from an old and uncertain gas lamp. She wrote in an inexpensive children's notebook (the famous "notebook" of two *sous*), and, in the course of a year, filled eighty-five pages with reminiscences of her childhood and early years of religious life. She never had any delusions that she was writing great literature, nor did she believe herself in possession of extraordinary literary talent. Some time later, writing to Père Roulland, she stated: "Told by a skillful pen, I think these details might interest you; but mine is not the pen to give charm to a long recital." At the trial, Pauline admitted: "I am convinced that the tremendous diffusion of the *Histoire* cannot be explained by the literary perfection of that work. It is not, as they say, great literature." Unfortunately, some of Thérèse's admirers have tried to treat her autobiography as if it were a work of literary genius. In actuality, it is only a hurriedly written epistolary document, composed in the language and style of the late Romantic era. But it is an astonishingly candid and frank report; and therein lies its charm and value—an honest exposition of a human experience.

At five o'clock in the evening of January 20, 1896, as

the nuns were assembling for prayer in the choir, Thérèse
quietly handed her manuscript to Pauline. The prioress
accepted it, but many months were to pass before she
even read it. Pauline testified that she apologized to Thérèse for her failure to read the manuscript, but the saint
was completely unconcerned about it. It had been another
of the many tasks imposed by religious obedience, faith-
fully undertaken, accomplished, and then forgotten.

After the difficult election of March 21, 1896, when
Mother Gonzague was restored to office, Pauline began to
read the manuscript casually. She placed no particular
importance on it at that time, regarding it as a family
souvenir to be read in the years to come. Such family souvenirs, some written by hand, others privately printed, are
fairly common in Europe, and can be found in the personal libraries even of families as insignificant as the
Martins of Lisieux. This genre of writing, so splendidly
satirized by J. P. Marquand in his *The Late George Apley,*
was the form in which Thérèse wrote; and as such, it was
preserved by Pauline. At the trial, the witnesses asked if
this sort of thing was usual in the Lisieux Carmel, and
they all testified that it was the first and only time it had
ever been done. When one of Thérèse's novices, Sister
Marie of the Trinity, asked permission to write her memoirs that she might record the graces God had given her,
Thérèse promptly refused. "It's better to keep the record
of God's favors in your memory than put them on paper,"
she said.

The second section of her manuscript was written between the thirteenth and sixteenth of September, 1896,
during the community retreat. Marie sent her a note asking her to write out some thoughts about "the secrets
Jesus had revealed to her," and added, pointedly, that
Mother Gonzague had given permission. In the four-day
period, Thérèse filled out ten closely written pages on or-

dinary white paper, and then gave them to her sister. This letter to Marie is an exposition of Thérèse's spiritual doctrine, and in the original printed editions of the autobiography it was placed as the concluding section of the book; in the unedited editions after 1956, it is placed in chronological order as the second manuscript.

The third section of the autobiography was written in the early summer of 1897, and addressed to Mother Gonzague. On the second of June, Pauline showed her family souvenir to Mother Gonzague for the first time, suggesting that something additional should be written because Thérèse had only covered the first years of her religious life in her manuscript. Pauline's cajoling approach to Mother Gonzague is rather unattractive, but it does illustrate how the nuns were forced to deal with the capricious prioress. She explained to Mother Gonzague the circumstances of the original composition, adding: ". . . but there is little in it to help you write her obituary after her death, because there is almost nothing about her religious life. If you commanded her, she could write something a little more serious, and I do not doubt that you would then have something of far greater value than I have." Mother Gonzague, obviously intrigued, issued the command to Thérèse, and even gave her a lined notebook of finer texture and quality than she had used before. Thérèse wrote the major part of this manuscript while sitting in a wheelchair under the row of chestnut trees in the convent garden. Her work suffered constant interruptions as the infirmarians busied themselves about her and the other nuns stopped to talk and ask her advice. "I don't think I wrote ten whole lines without interruption," she stated. The final pages were composed lying in bed in the infirmary, and the last page and a half is written in pencil. She had become too weak to continue dipping her pen in the ink bottle, and her pencil traveled across that last page in a weak and somewhat erratic scrawl. Her final written words were: ". . . I fly to Him through confidence and love."

She finished writing sometime in early July, and died on September 30. In the months following her death, the manuscripts were collected, prepared for publication, and released on September 30, 1898, exactly one year after her death. Two thousand copies were printed, and some of the nuns in the convent wondered how they could ever distribute so many.

In the year between Thérèse's death and the publication of her manuscripts, some radical editorial work was done on them. The critical edition of 1956 reveals that over seven thousand changes had been made in the text: some sections had been erased and written over, new passages not composed by Thérèse had been inserted, and some sections were entirely deleted—in fact, one third of the whole text had been cut before publication. This is the textual and critical problem that has confronted and annoyed some of Thérèse's biographers; this is the principal argument for the "pious fraud" theory.

Father Robo contends there was absolutely no justification for any revision of the manuscripts. "As one who has for years worked on original manuscripts, I must be forgiven if I maintain that no historical documents should ever be tampered with; I refuse absolutely to accept good intentions as a valid excuse for so-called 'improvements,'" he writes (p. 12). However, there were valid reasons for the editorial work, and they should be calmly considered.

First of all, there was Thérèse's own wish and directive that Pauline edit the manuscripts. The saint had not composed a finished work, and she knew it. The manuscripts contained faulty grammar, misspellings, repetitions, bad arrangement of material, and ideas poorly expressed. In fact, Thérèse had not written all the things she wanted to include, and she gave Pauline directives to add some specific material they had discussed in private conversations. About the time she was finishing the last manuscript, she said to Pauline: "I have not had time to write all that I wanted. It is not complete. Everything you find advisable to cut or add in the notebook I have written of my life, it is the same as if I had done the cutting and adding. Remember this later on, and don't have any scruples about the matter." She told Pauline to add the section about the sinner dying of love in the desert, which was dutifully inserted near the end of the 1898 edition. She asked Pauline to explain better her thought about confidence in God—"Make it quite clear, my mother, that even if I had committed every possible crime, I would still have the same confidence." And another time: "I've written about charity, but it's so badly written that I haven't expressed it as I wanted. But my thought is there. You'll have to correct it, because I assure you it's almost incomprehensible in places." About the justice of God: "My mother, I've barely said two words about God's justice in the notebook. But if you want, you'll find my thoughts fully explained in a letter I've written to Père Roulland."

Thérèse called Pauline "my biographer" (*mon historien*), and that fairly well explains the relationship between the two sisters in publishing the manuscript. Thérèse had not completed her literary task ("It is not finished," she said) and she commissioned Pauline to do it for her. Apart from the numerous erasures she made as she hurriedly composed, Thérèse did not have time to reread and correct her manuscript, nor did she ever see it as a whole work: she had given one section to Pauline, one to Marie, and another to Mother Gonzague, and only after her death were they collected and joined into one manuscript. According to Thérèse's express desires, therefore, Pauline was to serve as a literary collaborator, and not merely as an editor who would correct the spelling and bring clean copies to the printer. Abbé Combes, commenting on Pauline's editorial function, has found an analogy in some of the papal encyclicals when the Pope makes an outline of the material and then commissions someone to compose the actual document.[1] Whatever may be the precise literary term applied to Pauline's work, it is certain that she corrected the manuscript not as an officious meddler, but rather as one conscientiously fulfilling the mission entrusted to her by her dying sister. And we must remember the vital point ignored by the critics— that all of Thérèse's predictions about the publication of her memoirs and the consequent good they would accomplish refer not to the original manuscript, which was released only in 1956, but to the one she wanted Pauline to produce, the one she knew Pauline was going to produce from the notebooks.

Another factor influencing Pauline's actual editorial work rested on the basic character of the first manuscript, the one addressed to her. It was a family souvenir containing many intimate and rather uninteresting details of life in the Martin household. Many of these details were deleted; in fact, the major portion of the deletions occur in this section of the manuscript. Pauline's opinion of this manuscript is best ascertained by her remark to Mother Gonzague that she wanted Thérèse to write "something a little more serious." In deference to the Martin relatives mentioned in the manuscript, Pauline sent it to M. Guérin for his approval, which he readily gave; and we can presume that Thérèse's other sisters in the convent were asked if they had any objection to the publication of a family souvenir.

When Pauline approached Mother Gonzague to obtain her permission for publication, the prioress insisted that the manuscripts first be sent to Dom Godfrey Madelaine for correction and approbation. On the twenty-ninth of October, not even a month after Thérèse's death, Mother Gonzague herself wrote to Dom Madelaine, expressing her profound grief at the loss of Thérèse: "The death of our angel leaves a gap that will never be filled; the more I discover the perfections of that child of benediction, the more I regret having lost her." Then, in the same letter, she confided the existence of the manuscript to him: "Would you please correct it, or if your occupations prevent you, have someone else do it." A month later, Dom Madelaine received the manuscript, and he spent about three months studying it. March 1, 1898, he returned it to the convent with a letter addressed to Mother Gonzague. He had divided the manuscript into chapters, and marked various passages for deletion with a blue pencil. But his letter contained a number of editorial principles which Pauline was obliged to follow if she were going to have the memoirs published. Dom Madelaine said: "Everything in this manuscript is precious to you; but as far as the general public is concerned, there are details so intimate and so far above the ordinary level that I believe it would be better if you did not print them." He also spoke of errors in grammar and style, and indicated that there were a number of repetitious passages. Dom Godfrey testified at the trial that his actual corrections were few and did not affect the substance of the work; however, his editorial principles guided Pauline in making her revision of the manuscript. Dom Godfrey also rejected the various titles suggested by Pauline, and called it *The Story of a Soul*, the most fitting title it could possibly be given.

Another situation required Pauline to make additional

changes in the manuscript. Mother Gonzague insisted that the autobiography could only be published if it were made to look as if all three sections of Thérèse's memoirs were addressed to her, instead of just the final section. We are thus presented with some further unpleasant information about Mother Gonzague. We can find her action inexcusable, but Pauline, in 1897, found it undeniable, and she had to go through the manuscript, cutting and rearranging so that it appeared as if her sister had written it all to the prioress. After the printed version of the memoirs appeared, Mother Gonzague became afraid that her action in the publication of the book would be revealed—the addressing of the other two sections of the manuscript to her; and the many things suppressed because "they would displease her"—and she prepared to destroy the original documents. To prevent this, Pauline laboriously copied the corrections that Mother Gonzague's attitude had dictated into the original manuscript, and thus prevented its destruction. (Those critics who maintain that one of Pauline's purposes in editing the manuscript was to disparage Mother Gonzague, seem to forget that Mother Gonzague was prioress at the time of publication. She supervised the entire operation, and even had the manuscript read aloud to the entire community. Knowing what we do about the erratic prioress, it seems highly improbable that she would have permitted any editing which could be interpreted, even if only by the nuns of Lisieux, as unflattering.)

These are the reasons for Pauline's editorial work, reasons so urgent that she had to make her corrections and additions. Father Robo talks about an "historical document," but we must remember that in 1897 Thérèse's notebooks were hardly regarded as historical documents: they were only a nun's hurriedly written memoirs, the first draft of a book she wanted Pauline to produce. There are

very few books published exactly as they are written—
publishers and experienced writers will testify to that.
Some books are edited lightly, a sentence structure here,
a punctuation mark there; others are heavily edited with
massive changes in the text, as Maxwell Perkins did for
Thomas Wolfe's books. But no one accuses an editor of
"tampering with historical documents" when he works on
a manuscript.

Rather than criticism, Pauline would seem to deserve
praise for her editorial work. Had she not made the corrections, then surely the autobiography would not have
been published at that time. Had she attempted to publish the rambling, personal memoir of a recently deceased
nun exactly as it was written, she would not have received
the required ecclesiastical permission. Even at that, the
Bishop of Lisieux—Msgr. Hugonin, from whom Thérèse
had sought admission to Carmel—was hesitant about
granting permission. "You have to be careful of women's
imagination," he said to Dom Madelaine. Reluctantly, he
gave his consent, but refused to write a preface for the
book. And Pauline testified at the trial that some Carmelite convents were displeased when they received the
printed version. "This life was infantile, and not at all in
harmony with the austerity of Carmel," the Carmel de
l'Avenue de Messine in Paris wrote back.

The publication of St. Thérèse's autobiography, therefore, must not be studied as if it were a book published
some fifty or sixty years after her death. It must be
studied in the actual historical context—the Lisieux of
1897, when within a month after Thérèse's death, her sister gathered together the two notebooks and the five
sheets of writing to prepare them for publication.

But the larger and more important question remains:
did the revisions distort the portrait of St. Thérèse or her
doctrine?

The issue was of concern to the ecclesiastical judges during the trial of 1910, and they demanded that both versions of the autobiography be produced. Pauline restored the corrections made because of Mother Gonzague, and delivered the original manuscript to the trial; thus the judges had the opportunity of studying the original document against the printed version. They read both versions carefully, comparing one against the other, studying them line by line, and they discovered no essential difference between the two texts. The only objection made by the judges concerned the fusion of the three original manuscripts into one, and the corrections which made it appear as if Thérèse had written all three of them to Mother Gonzague. The judges asked that future editions be revised so that the division be indicated and the three sections be addressed to the proper persons; this included the restoration of some material which had been specifically addressed to Pauline or Marie. The Roman censor gave his *Nihil Obstat* in 1912, and the editions of the autobiography from 1914 incorporated these revisions.

This should have ended the discussion. But, amazingly, it did not. Some critics still maintain the fraud theory, claiming that the real image of Thérèse was not discovered until 1956, when the original manuscript was released. They therefore find themselves in a peculiar position. They must contend that Pauline distorted the image of Thérèse and her doctrine, and that the Congregation of Rites discovered this fraud during the process of canonization but yet tacitly gave permission for further dissemination of the error. This is a position which is as uncomfortable as it is dangerous.

To silence the critics, Msgr. Lemmonier, Bishop of Bayeux and Lisieux, wrote a special preface (*L'Avis*) for the 1924 edition of the autobiography. He lamented the charges which were being made, and categorically stated that the edited texts "absolutely show us her soul" (*nous livrent absolument son âme*), and give us a "true and finished portrait" of St. Thérèse. And he reminded the reader that the tribunal of canonization had compared the two versions of the autobiography, and had found that the changes "did not affect the fundamental truth of the published texts."[2]

Still, the irresponsible criticism continued, and we had to wait until 1956 to see the basis of the decision by the Roman authorities. Then, comparing the two texts, scholars agreed that both versions of the autobiography are substantially the same. This is the opinion of Père François in his introduction to the definitive edition of the manuscripts: "Without a doubt, the content of the narrative and the essence of the doctrine remain obviously the same."[3] Père Philip of the Trinity, a consultor to the Holy Office in Rome, stated in *Ephemerides Carmeliticae:* "We say that the doctrine is exactly the same. We have not seen any new doctrine in the photostatic text."[4] The Spanish scholar, Padre Baldomero Duque, rector of the seminary at Avila, says: "Actually, the Thérèse of *The Story of a Soul* and the Thérèse of the photostatic manuscripts is the same, exactly the same."[5] And Padre Duque, discussing the veneration given to Thérèse all these years since her canonization, raises a thoughtful point: "God does not deceive men, nor is He even able to deceive them."

To discuss all the objections of the critics would entail a line-by-line evaluation of the text, and that is beyond the scope of this book. But we might indicate some of the major elements of Pauline's editorial work in the areas of omissions, additions, and corrections. Despite the expectation of an exposé, the omitted sections prove to be singularly unexciting. Père François has made a list of all the omissions of more than one line; of the 420 omitted passages, 310 concern Thérèse's childhood. The most informative of the deleted sections are the passages where Thérèse says she had trouble reciting the rosary without distractions, and her violation of the friars' cloister in Italy. But most of the passages are simple details of the Martin family—for example, Thérèse's comment that, as a child, she preferred not to have visitors when she was sick because they sat around her bed "like a row of onions." We find some precedent for this kind of editorial work in the case of St. Teresa of Avila: her writings were corrected by Padre Luis de Leon, who deleted many references to people still alive at the time; it was only a number of years after St. Teresa's death that the omitted sections were restored.

Pauline's additions to the text are of different kinds. Some are things Thérèse specifically told her to add. Others are details Pauline knew by personal experience or which Thérèse related to her—for example, the wound of love, which was not written by Thérèse but told to Pauline on a number of occasions. Others are only additional details to fill out an episode related by Thérèse. And, finally, some are details about Thérèse's doctrine taken from the notes Sister Marie of the Trinity made during Thérèse's conferences to the novices. For this reason, the edited version of the manuscript will always be valuable, because it supplies us with biographical data about Thérèse which, added to her own autobiographical sections, gives us a more complete picture.

Pauline's corrections are chiefly concerned with giving the text a more accurate reading. Thus, the punctuation and grammar are corrected. But some episodes are revised when Thérèse's memory fails her—for example, in the audience with Pope Leo XIII, she states that her fa-

ther approached the Pope after her; the official records,
and Céline's recollections, show that her father preceded
her, and was out of the chamber when Thérèse knelt at
the Pope's feet. The correction most frequently cited by
the critics is the phrase Thérèse quotes from her mother's
letter about her when she was two years old—"she is a
nervous child," Mme. Martin wrote; and Pauline corrected it to "exuberant child."

It is difficult to determine with any precision Pauline's
exact mentality in her editorial work. Assuredly, a nun's
sense of propriety regulated some of the changes—the nun
who annoyed Thérèse in the choir by scraping her fingernail along her teeth is made to jangle her rosary instead.
Also, Thérèse's occasional bits of irony and flashes of humor are carefully deleted from this personal account of a
nun printed in the 1890's.

But a careful study of the *whole* text does not support
the thesis that Pauline tried to delete Thérèse's faults and
make her as perfect as possible. First, in Pauline's edited
version, the whole story of Thérèse's difficulties is recounted: her childhood stubbornness when she refused
to kiss the ground for the penny; her vanity with the
sleeveless dress; her "self-love"; her sensitivity; her shyness; her tears; her scruples; her strange illness; her difficulties in the convent; her reprimands from Mother
Gonzague when she did her work inadequately; her
temptations against faith. All of those details are included
in the text produced by Pauline, and their inclusion—
sometimes at great length and with many details—hardly
sounds like the efforts of a nun trying to hide her sister's
faults. Furthermore, some of Pauline's deletions show that
she was clearly not motivated by a desire to show her sister in the best light. In one of Mme. Martin's letters which
Thérèse included in her manuscript, the young child is

shown sitting quietly for two or three hours, not moving while she waited for her sister. It is a fine example of young Thérèse's control, but Pauline deleted it. Again, one of the most telling proofs that Thérèse was not a spoiled child is the section relating how she refused to play off Pauline against her father, and how she obeyed Pauline even when she knew she could approach her father for a more favorable judgment. Pauline deleted this whole section. We can never really ascertain why Pauline deleted these texts; but had her paramount desire in editing the manuscript been to show her sister's virtues and hide her defects, as the critics maintain, then surely these passages should not have been deleted—especially since they disprove facts she was supposed to be hiding: the nervous child, and the spoiled child.

In comparing the edited text of Thérèse's autobiography with the unedited version released in 1956, we must remember that we are not comparing a genuine text with a spurious or faked one. Thérèse wanted Pauline ("my biographer") to produce an edited version of what she had written, with the understanding that the final result would be part autobiography and part biography. We are delighted to have the unedited version now, because it supplies us with additional facts about Thérèse—just as the edited version of Pauline supplies facts not contained in the original. But Pauline's version was, in God's plan, the one used to spread Thérèse's message throughout the world. Pope Benedict XV said: "Without the world-wide circulation of The Story of a Soul, this mission could not have been accomplished." And Thérèse said that her autobiography "would accomplish much good for souls." However, both these statements, as well as Thérèse's many prophecies, refer to the edition prepared by Pauline. We must, if nothing else, respect God's plan.

2. THE PHOTOGRAPHS

There are extant, today, forty-five actual photographs taken of Thérèse during her lifetime, plus two additional photographs taken of the body before burial. The presentation and diffusion of these photographs has been the source of another controversy about St. Thérèse.

At the outset, it is important to remember that the issue of the photographs is one entirely distinct from that of the manuscript. Thérèse made no predictions whatsover about the photographs, nor did she ever request their distribution. The judges at the trial did not ask to examine them, and, of course, they made no decision at all about them. Thérèse's manuscript was to be the means of spreading her message and person; thus, she had no concern beyond that, nor did the ecclesiastical judges. The photographs are a secondary and incidental question.

Father Robo tries to combine the two issues into one, suggesting that there was "a parallel treatment of idealization" between the photos and the manuscript (p. 36). Thus, what was done in the photographs must have been done in the manuscript, and vice versa. This is, simply, one of the bad arguments intelligent men make.

After Thérèse's death, the Carmel found itself in possession of forty-seven photographs, and there were apparently a few others that were lost when they were sent to other convents for viewing. Four of these photographs were taken before she entered the Carmel, two were taken when she was a novice, and the rest during the last three years of her life. Only the early photographs were taken by a professional photographer; the two of Thérèse as a novice were taken by Abbé Gombault, who entered the cloister, with permission, to help the nuns install gas light; the remaining pictures were taken by the nuns themselves. Céline brought a camera with her when she

entered Carmel, and after some initial reluctance, the
nuns began to use it. The majority of the photographs
show Thérèse in a group with some of the other nuns.

In the early editions of the autobiography, photographs
of Thérèse were used as illustrations, and only in later
editions were the romanticized paintings employed. (This
seems to be a fact unknown by the critics.) The 1902
edition contained a photograph of Thérèse sitting med-
itatively in the convent cemetery. This is an actual and
unretouched photo, except that it was originally part of a
group photo of five nuns; Thérèse's picture was cut from
the group and superimposed on a picture of the cemetery.
In this well-known photograph, her face is sad, and has
an almost bulldog look about it. The same photograph was
retouched in the 1910 edition, so that the face is more
oval, the expression more bland. The 1902 edition also
contained a photo of Thérèse's body lying in the choir
three days after her death. The head is circled with a
crown of flowers, the face turned slightly to the side so
that it presents a three-quarter view; the features are
somewhat haggard and drawn. This photo was only
slightly retouched, just enough to emphasize the existing
features. After 1906, the photo was not used in subse-
quent editions of the autobiography.[6]

The Carmel, therefore, first released unretouched, or
slightly retouched, photographs of St. Thérèse. But after
1906, the thinking at the Carmel changed radically, and
a series of sentimental and romantic paintings took their
place; and the greater part of the photographs released
by the nuns were seriously retouched so that her head
was rounded into a perfect oval, and her features became
vacantly serene, inert, and insipid. We can only regret
that the actual photos, no matter how inexpert, were re-
placed by these meaningless and horrendus products of
late Romantic art. While no apology can be given for the

Carmel's decision, we do have the obligation of trying to find the reason for the change.

The Carmel of Lisieux has always maintained that Thérèse took a poor picture. There would seem to be some truth to this when we study the forty-seven actual photographs. There is a great dissimilarity of expression and features among the photos, even of those taken a few minutes apart. The explanation lies in the primitive photographic equipment used in the 1890's. All of the photos were posed, and it was necessary to maintain the pose during an exposure time of seven to nine seconds. Thérèse, we are told by the nuns, had extremely mobile features, and during the seven-second exposure time her face would often take on a different cast. Added to this was the fact that this primitive and bulky equipment was employed by amateurs—the cloistered nuns, mostly. Thérèse's sisters claimed that the most accurate photograph of the saint was the one taken by the Lisieux photographer, Mme. Besnier, in April of 1888, a few days before her entrance to Carmel. (That photograph is reproduced with others, in the section of illustrations following p. 120.) The 1888 photo shows Thérèse wearing her hair on top of her head; this was the first time she had worn it that way since her visit to the Bishop, when she rearranged her hair to make herself appear older. Thérèse's sisters add, however, that photo makes her hair look much darker than its actual blond color.

A more fundamental reason for the retouching of the photos and the substitution of paintings was the artistic mood of the era. People preferred the painting to the photograph—and this was particularly true for the nuns of Lisieux, who considered Thérèse's photos to be poor ones. The general thinking of the era was that a better and more penetrating likeness was obtained by a painting than by any amount of photography, a relatively new and uncertain science. The problem was that the only art those people appreciated was the pompous, idealistic art of late Romanticism. The impressionism of Paris had no appeal for these people, nor did realism; and certainly a later surrealism would have proved unattractive to them. They were committed to idealism in art—and it seemed to be a fitting vehicle, because unfortunately so much of ecclesiastical art seems permanently stalled in the baroque period.

In 1911, Canon Dubosq, one of the official promoters of the cause, asked Céline to do a portrait of Thérèse which symbolized her spiritual life. Céline then painted her well-known "Thérèse of the Roses," and when one of the saint's former novices, Sister Marie Magdalen, saw it she stated: "It's just like I'm looking at her again." This almost unbelievable statement can only be explained by the artistic values of the era: people were not looking for realism in art, but only symbolism—and at that, a symbolism and idealism of the most stiff and affected kind.

Canon Dubosq also advised the nuns to have enlargements of the photographs made and then retouch them.[7] Thus, the first suggestion for retouching came not from the nuns but from Canon Dubosq, promoter of the cause and rector of the major seminary in Bayeux. When the nuns turned their hand to retouching the photos, they applied the same artistic principles they used in the paintings. This is particularly evident in the 1889 photograph by Abbé Gombault, which they felt was an especially poor photo and badly in need of retouching. Sister Marie of the Trinity has said: "The retouched photographs give a better understanding of St. Thérèse than do any of the actual photographs." And once again, we reach the impasse of late Romantic artistic values!

One thing seems quite certain, however. There was no intention of fraud or deceit on the part of the nuns. As we have seen, they published original photos of St. Thérèse in the early editions of the autobiography. And from time to time they continued to issue unretouched photos, although they clearly favored the retouched ones. Thus, in 1926 the Carmel issued an unretouched photograph of Thérèse taken when she was twenty-two. (Reproduced in this book on p. 120.) It shows a full-faced, robust nun before her consumption began to emaciate her. The only correction made in this photo was the removal of some white dots on the picture, imperfections caused by the negative. In 1933, the Carmel released the intriguing picture of Thérèse doing the wash in the laundry, another unretouched photo. And in 1956, as a frontispiece to the unedited version of the manuscript, they released a picture of a gaunt, sickly looking Thérèse taken after her first consumptive attack (p. 120). Most of these pictures, as we noted, are detail photos selected from a group picture of nuns.

The discussion of the photographs ends nowhere—except with the possible reiteration that Romantic art is inferior art. Fortunately, in the early part of 1961, the Carmel of Lisieux released its entire dossier of photographs of St. Thérèse, and we now have the opportunity of viewing all the original photographs.

3. THE CAUSE

Pope Pius XI called it a "hurricane of glory" (*ouragan de gloire*). And, indeed, it was—a reaction from all over the world, a ground swell of praise, a litany of gratitude for the miracles.

The autobiography ran through edition after edition. Between 1898 and 1915, over two hundred thousand copies of the French edition were published, and seven hundred thousand copies of the abridged French edition. By 1917, it had been translated into thirty-four languages or dialects. Requests poured into the Carmel for relics, pictures, anything connected with Thérèse. The nuns distributed over eight million pictures of Thérèse during those first years, and soon almost every conceivable relic was gone—clothes, bed linen, articles used by Thérèse, all divided up in small fragments and sent throughout the world.

The Carmel became deluged with a flood of letters. Up to 1911, it averaged around fifty a day, and in the following years it grew to two, three, and four hundred a day. After 1914, it was as much as five hundred letters a day.

And the shower of roses began. Reports began to trickle back to Lisieux of favors granted through the intercession of Thérèse. There were stories of cures and restoration to health, some of them amazing and inexplicable things. But even more moving were the stories of the spiritual transformations, the lives radically changed by reading Thérèse's autobiography, the new religious convictions stimulated by the simple words of the young Carmelite nun.

During the First World War, Thérèse became the darling of the troops in the French trenches. And after the War, other soldiers demonstrated their gratitude by donating altars in the chapel of the Lisieux Carmel: the altar of St. Michael was donated by Irish soldiers, St. Joseph by Canadian soldiers, and St. Teresa by American soldiers. Votive plaques of gratitude for favors received were sent to the chapel, and soon the walls were covered with them; they came from India, Brazil, Egypt, Chile, Italy, Belgium, Trinidad, Algeria.

In Rome, Pope Benedict XV dispensed with the usual fifty-year waiting period, and allowed the investigations to be started for Thérèse's beatification. Pope Pius XI told

Msgr. de Teil, Vice Postulator of the cause: "This cause must be completed quickly!" And the Cardinal-Prefect of the Congregation of Rites stated that if the cause were not completed quickly, she would be canonized by the voice of the people.

In the midst of this hurricane, one interesting question presents itself: did the nuns at Lisieux expect all this? Did they realize Thérèse was a saint? We know that a segment of the community had little intimate knowledge of her. One nun, Sister Vincent de Paul, wondered whatever could possibly be said about her in an obituary notice. Thérèse was, for this segment, a pious little nun, devout, prayerful, quite sweet and charming. The other segment, particularly the novices, had a more profound respect for her holiness; they had seen her operate at closer quarters; they knew her. Pauline was in the closest association with her during the last four or five months of her life, and she, if anyone, could be expected to have the clearest ideas about Thérèse's possible sanctity. Undoubtedly, Pauline knew that the autobiography would accomplish a great deal of good; Thérèse had predicted it, and her sister believed her. And she was also aware of Thérèse's virtue and holiness. But the possibility of Thérèse's future canonization never seemed to have crossed her mind. At the trial, she testified:

> I truly regarded her as a saint, especially during her last illness. However, I did not dream that one day her canonization would be considered, since I thought there would have to be miracles and extraordinary happenings in her life for that.

Pauline gives similar testimony elsewhere at the trial, and she says, somewhat wonderingly, that Thérèse's simple, uneventful life did not resemble most of the canonized saints in the Church. Pauline was apparently laboring under the common delusion that extraordinary events are necessary for the proof of heroic sanctity. Thérèse, then, had a message for her own sister, as well as for the rest of the world.[8]

Thus, when the nuns of Lisieux sent out the first printed copies of the autobiography in 1898, they were not trying to lay the groundwork for a campaign to promote Thérèse's canonization. Thérèse had convinced Pauline that her manuscript was important, that it would accomplish much good; and Pauline, in turn, had convinced Mother Gonzague. The prioress agreed to have the manuscript printed, under the conditions she specified, and then mailed to other Carmelite convents in lieu of the usual obituary notice. It is important to note that the original edition of the autobiography was not published and issued for general distribution; it was privately printed and distributed only to other cloistered Carmelite convents. Apart from the few negative reactions we have noted, the book was enthusiastically received. The other convents loaned the book to priests and friends, and wrote to Lisieux for more copies. Soon people who had read or heard of the book began to demand copies, and the original edition of two thousand copies was quickly depleted. The Carmel then issued a general edition and the publishing phenomenon occurred: edition after edition went through the press until the total copies numbered in the millions.

Ida Goerres sees something sinister in all this.[9] While she admits that the ultimate explanation of Thérèse's popularity must rest in God's designs, she still charges the nuns with organizing "a vast propaganda apparatus" and employing "the magic of publicity and advertising" (p. 394). She writes: "Here, too, we must be amazed at the unconscious sureness with which these nuns, who after all were entirely ignorant of all advertising methods, found precisely the right way to impress their beloved Thérèse upon the attention and imagination of the rest of the world" (p. 392). Once again, this is the same charge made forty years ago by the Devil's Advocate, a charge examined and dismissed by the Congregation of Rites. It is a serious charge which was carefully examined, because the Holy See is extremely sensitive to any kind of program to stimulate artificial interest in a possible saint. One popular cause of this century was abruptly terminated, purportedly because the relatives of the candidate were organizing too intense a campaign.

The judges at the trial asked the nuns about the publicity emanating from the Carmel of Lisieux, the pictures, the relics, the medals. Sister Thérèse of St. Augustine said: "We have done nothing to excite this enthusiasm. All that the Carmel has done or published has been done in reply to the pressing demands of the people. And we get many more requests than we can answer." Sister Marie of the Trinity also testified: "I am in charge of the arrangements with the manufacturers of these images and medallions. I can affirm in all truth that these have been produced only to answer the spontaneous requests we received, and even at that we cannot satisfy them all." Pauline stated that no arrangements were ever inaugurated by the Carmel for translations of the autobiography; requests for translation rights were received, and the permission granted. The Paris Jesuit, Père Auriault, who was well acquainted with the community at Lisieux after Thérèse's death, stated at the trial: "Nothing has been done to create her reputation of sanctity . . . The means of publicity employed by the Carmel of Lisieux has a relationship to this reputation of effect to cause rather than cause to effect."

The response to the Devil's Advocate is one of the most impassioned sections of the whole trial. Msgr. Toeschi said:

> No sane person would see this reputation as deriving from any natural cause . . . There is no equation between the cause and the effect. How else can you explain the tremendous approval, the translation of the manuscript into so many languages, the effect it has had on souls, the results of piety and fervor. No prudent man would ascribe that to a human cause . . . Truly, to move the hearts of men, to influence their wills, to correct people's lives, to excite vocations to the cloister, to increase the love of God and men, to teach the ways of the Lord—man could never do this without the power of Divine help and favor.

As Thérèse herself said, God alone was the One who would accomplish her mission. To appreciate that, one would have to stand in the streets of Lisieux some quiet day and try to imagine the town some sixty years ago. A young nun had just died of tuberculosis. The convent was preparing to send out her personal memoirs—not to bookstores, nor potential buyers, nor even to magazines and newspapers for review, but to other cloistered convents! Even a Madison Avenue agency would be hard-pressed to develop something out of a situation like that. It is just one more proof of God's stamp of approval on her life, her doctrine, and her mission.

The hurricane of glory reached its most intense peak in the 1920's. The miracles selected for her beatification and canonization were presented to the Congregation, and the clamor for that final honor continued throughout the Catholic world. Then, on May 17, 1925, Thérèse was formally canonized by Pope Pius XI. During the homily of the Mass in the Basilica of St. Peter's, the Pope said: "We earnestly desire that all the faithful carefully study her so that they might imitate her by becoming little children, since, according to the words of Christ, there is no other was to reach the Kingdom of Heaven."

Not quite thirty-eight years before, Thérèse had quietly knelt to pray in that same Basilica during her pilgrimage to Rome; now she was being proclaimed a saint there. She was Thérèse of Lisieux—but now she belonged to the world.

CHAPTER VIII

THE GLORY

Today, some sixty years after her death, St. Thérèse's story has circled the world. Her statue is found in towering stone cathedrals and in small wooden chapels, in the heartlands of Christianity and in pagan mission territories, in public shrines and in private homes. New editions of her autobiography are constantly being run through the presses, and they are read with undiminishing enthusiasm by priests and laymen, teen-agers and older people, the lettered and the uninstructed. Miracles of every description—the promised shower of roses—are still reported from every part of the globe, and their list seems unending.

The Popes, over the decades that separate us from her, have said some amazing things about St. Thérèse. One called her the greatest saint of modern times, another said she had the secret of sanctity for the whole world, and another stated that if her doctrine were put into practice it would reshape and reform our entire society.

The hurricane of glory continues.

But there is an astonishing disproportion between the reaction accorded the young French saint and the simple, almost prosaic character of her life. Saints of greater his-

torical importance and greater personal heroism have
been less extolled, less loved. St. Clare, St. Jane Frances
de Chantal, St. Louise de Marillac, for example, all of
them founders of religious orders, made a stronger im-
pact on the world in which they lived and were themselves more vigorous personalities who were capable of
attracting a band of followers; and yet no one of these
attractive and inspiring saints received the praise and
endorsement accorded Thérèse Martin.

This, then, is the basic enigma of St. Thérèse's case: the
contrast between the glory—the miracles, the amazing
accolades of the Popes, the world-wide enthusiasm—and
the undramatic and routine fabric of her life.

It cannot be solved by attempting to make Thérèse
what she was not, by attempting to write drama and pathos into her life, by making her a tragic figure in rebellion
against the world outside her and within her. Nor can it
be solved by sentimentalizing about her, by portraying
her as an ethereal, rosy-cheeked creature living in a
dream world of sweetness and light. She was none of these
things: she was only an ordinary person in ordinary human situations. And therein lies the solution to the
enigma: she has been loved, praised, and proposed for
our imitation because she makes sanctity comprehensible,
she reduces it to terms we know and understand. The
theory and the doctrine in the teachings of the saints and
spiritual writers finds articulation and accomplishment in
her life, and in a way that is readily intelligible and ob-
servable. In studying her life, we cannot possibly be dis-
tracted by historical greatness, nor can we confuse the
essential message of sanctity with the outstanding accom-
plishments the saints sometimes achieve.

St. Thérèse called herself a "little soul," and we must
understand that phrase in its most literal meaning: she
was a little soul, involved, as most of us are, in an ordinary

and unspectacular life. The experiences of her life were common, unnoticed by the world in which she lived. Even her sufferings, as intense and aggravating as they were to her, resemble the ordinary misfortunes of good people anywhere in the world: her mother died, she became shy and upset easily, she was struck down with a crippling illness, she had to watch her father disintegrating before her eyes, she was plunged into the darkness of the spiritual life, she was bewildered by temptations against faith, she wasted away of tuberculosis. She once confessed that her greatest physical suffering in the convent was the dampness and chill caused by the creek that ran outside the convent wall—and from that statement we can discern the tempo of her life. Observing her, we can observe ourselves; and—the vital message!—we can see how we ourselves can become saints within the structure of our own lives.

Dom Godfrey's title for Thérèse's autobiography, *The Story of a Soul,* is as precise and appropriate as it could possibly be, for that is exactly what it is: the chronicle of a soul's growth in holiness, a chronicle written with unbelievable clarity. We can watch Thérèse, from her earliest years, taking determined steps toward God as she decided to refuse Him nothing. We can witness her growth in union with Him, her continuing experience with Him. We see her faults and her achievements, her happinesses and her sorrows. We observe the most constant practice of the virtues worked out in the fabric of ordinary, human situations. And we see it all culminate in her dying gasp, "My God, I love you"—an epitome of her whole life. Perhaps never before in the history of Christendom have we had so complete and excellent an opportunity to witness the story of a soul, the interior growth into sanctity.

She achieved sanctity, Pope Pius XI said, without going

beyond the common order of things, and a careful study of her life bears this out. There is no reason why this should be a startling fact, but it is for many people, presumably because of the distorted notion of sanctity they have acquired. This leads to that almost inevitable temptation to describe her life from a negative viewpoint, insisting that she was *not* this or she was *not* that. But such an approach to Thérèse's life and doctrine does her a disservice, for her doctrine is an eminently positive one. The simplicity of her life only serves to separate the essential from the inessential.

Not only does St. Thérèse present a positive program for sanctity, but she presents it in the clearest and simplest manner. "Sanctity does not consist in this or that practice," she said, "but rather in a disposition of the heart which makes us humble and small in the arms of God." She has no complicated method or procedure to teach us, no involved processes, only a firm insistence that sanctity consists in meeting God, knowing Him, loving Him, obeying Him. "She has taken the mathematics out of sanctity," Cardinal Bourne said of her in his frequently quoted phrase.

Her Little Way, that program of life endorsed so strongly by the Popes, is an articulation of her own personal experience with God. She discovered God, and she wants to share that discovery with us. She experienced the Mercy of God, His understanding, His compassion— and, most of all, His Love. She once wrote to her cousin, Marie Guérin: "You want a means for reaching perfection. I know of only one: Love." Her whole life is a response to God's Love, and everything in her life is caught up in one gigantic, loving thrust toward Him.

In the July before her death, she said: "I feel that my mission is about to begin: my mission of making souls love God as I love Him, of teaching my Little Way to souls."

St. Thérèse has been faithful to her mission, she has been teaching souls to love God. And that is the ultimate explanation for the hurricane of glory—God is calling attention to her imperishable message, the simple and moving invitation to sanctity.

The search for St. Thérèse, therefore, terminates not in the Normandy of the 1890's, but it terminates wherever her autobiography is read, wherever her story is told; because when we discover Thérèse, we discover ourselves, we discover what we could be, what we should be . . . what we can be.

NOTES

GENERAL NOTE I:

In quoting the opinions of those who propose the distorted-image theory, I have, for the most part, directed my attention to two specific books. This is a decision I have reached after much reflection, and it is based chiefly on two considerations. First, there are so many books and articles proposing the theory that it would be difficult and repetitious to make any attempt at citing and discussing them in a book of this size. Secondly, many of the books are not available in this country or in this language(the most popular and influential book of this school, in fact, is *La Petite Sainte Thérèse* by Maxence van der Meersch, which has never been translated into English), and quotations from a number of unavailable sources would be of small value to an American audience. However, my decision to address myself principally to two books does not imply that I must ignore any significant arguments or questions raised, for there is a definite similarity between the arguments presented, whether it be in English, French, or German; it is a similarity of reasoning and expression which, at first, seems to lend a new authenticity to the authors' claims, but it is such a marked similarity that closer study leads one to a slight suspicion about it. There are, of course, divergent opinions within the school itself, as I have indicated, but I feel that a representation of all the important thinking about the supposed fraud at Lisieux is contained in the two books I have selected.

The books: *Two Portraits of St. Teresa of Lisieux* by Etienne Robo, and *The Hidden Face* by Ida Goerres. Both books are well written and stimulating, and they have both enjoyed a wide reading here in America. Father Robo's book is more polemic and argumentative, written with the fire and occasional irascibility which make that kind of reading exciting and absorbing. Frau Goerres' book is more calm, but yet more perspicacious and rewarding, probing carefully into the life of St. Thérèse with fine psychological insight. (However, I feel the Goerres book to be the more dangerous, since it relies on some unfortunate principles which have been criticized by European theologians, but seem to have escaped the notice of many people on this side of the Atlantic.)

GENERAL NOTE II:

Unless otherwise identified, all statements of the witnesses in this book are quoted directly from their sworn testimony at the trial, as contained in the *Processus*, the summary of testimony at the trial for canonization. The *Processus*, a massive quarto volume of some 1300 pages, is a largely unavailable document; there are only a few copies in print, for the most part zealously guarded in European libraries, and, therefore, inaccessible to the general reader or student. We have decided to omit references and page citations through the course of this book so as not to clog the text with multiple references to an unavailable document. The official title of the *Processus* is: *Bajocensis et Lexoviensis Beatificationis et Canonizationis Servae Dei Sororis Theresiae a Puero Jesu Monialis Professae Ordinis Carmelitarum Excalceatorum in Monasterio Lexoviensi Positio Super Virtutibus* (Rome: 1920).

Statements from St. Thérèse's autobiography are quoted from *Manuscrits Autobiographiques de Sainte Thérèse de L'Enfant-Jésus* (Lisieux: Carmel of Lisieux, 1956).

INTRODUCTION

1. Lancelot C. Sheppard, "The Story of a Soul," *The Tablet* (London: Sept. 22, 1956), pp. 224–225.
2. Etienne Robo, *Two Portraits of St. Teresa of Lisieux* (Westminster: Newman Press, 1957), p. 47.
3. *Ibid.*, p. 48.
4. Ida Friederike Goerres, *The Hidden Face* (New York: Pantheon, 1959), p. 393.
5. Discourse of Pope Benedict XV, Aug. 14, 1921 on the occasion of the *Super Dubio* decree. An English translation of the discourse was published in a small pamphlet by Desclee de Brouwer: Lille, 1922. The actual *Super Dubio* decree is given in *AAS*, XIII (1921), pp. 449–452.
6. Homily at the Mass of Canonization, May 17, 1925. *AAS*, XVII (1925), pp. 211–214.
7. *AAS*, XXXXVI (1945), p. 404.

CHAPTER I REFLECTIONS ON THE FACTS

1. Père François de Sainte-Marie, O.C.D., *Manuscrits Autobiographiques de Sainte Thérèse de L'Enfant-Jésus* (Lisieux: Carmel of Lisieux, 1956), Tome I, II, and III.
2. *Ibid.*, Tome I, pp. 75–78.

3. Hans Urs von Balthasar, *Thérèse of Lisieux* (New York: Sheed and Ward, 1954), p. xxiii.
4. *Ibid.*, p. xxiv.
5. *Ibid.*, pp.276–277.
6. *Ibid.*, p. 277.
7. Cf. Nicolau and Salaverri, *Sacrae Theologiae Summa* (Madrid: Biblioteca de Autores Cristianos, 1955), pp. 741–742.
8. *AAS*, XVII (1925), p. 347.
9. *AAS*, XXVI (1934), p. 540.

CHAPTER II THE CHILD

1. Stéphane-Joseph Piat, O.F.M., *The Story of a Family* (New York: P. J. Kenedy & Sons, 1947), p. 25.
2. *Ibid.*, pp. 176–177.
3. *Ibid.*, pp. 178–179.
4. *AAS*, XV (1923), pp. 202–207.
5. Goerres, *op. cit.*, pp. 28, 31, 41, 82.
6. Translation of *Miserentissimus Deus* quoted from Louis Verheylezoon, S.J., *Devotion to the Sacred Heart* (Westminster: Newman Press, 1955), p. 4.
7. Translation from *The Pope Speaks*, vol. 1, no. 3, p. 212; Cf. *AAS* XXXXVI (1954).
8. Goerres, *op. cit.*, pp. 415–416.
9. John Beevers, *Storm of Glory* (New York: Doubleday-Image, 1955), p. 24.
10. Piat, *op. cit.*, p. 245.
11. Jean Guitton, *The Spiritual Genius of St. Thérèse* (Westminster: Newman Press, 1958), pp. 13–14.

CHAPTER III GROWTH AND ILLUMINATION

1. Thomas Verner Moore, *Heroic Sanctity and Insanity* (New York: Grune & Stratton, 1959), pp. 217–218.
2. Père Marie-Eugene de L'Enfant-Jésus, O.C.D., "La Grace De Noël 1886 Chez Ste. Thérèse de l'Enfant-Jésus," *Carmel*, II, (1959) pp. 99–100.
3. Padre Alberto Barrios Moneo, C.M.F., *La Espiritualidad de Santa*

Teresa de Lisieux (Madrid: S. Corazón de Jesus, 1958) pp. 127–144.

4. Père François, *op. cit.*, II, p .18.
5. *Ibid.*, p. 26.
6. Cf. *Spiritual Life* (Milwaukee: Vol. II, no. 1, March, 1959) pp. 57–58.
7. Père Marie-Eugene, *op. cit.*, p. 108.
8. Teresa of Avila, *Life*, Ch. XXVII.

CHAPTER IV EVALUATION

1. From an address of Pope Pius XII to participants in the National Congress of Professional Nurses and Assistant Health Visitors, Oct. 1, 1953. Reported in *L'Osservatore Romano*, Oct. 2, 1953; and *AAS*, XXXXV (1953), p. 726.
2. Gabriel of St. Mary Magdalen, "Present Norms of Holiness" in *Conflict and Light* (New York: Sheed and Ward, 1953), p. 167.
3. Richard P. Vaughan, S.J., "Neuroticism and Perfection," *Review for Religious* (March, 1960) pp. 93–101.
4. Cf. *Spiritual Life, loc. cit.*
5. Luke, 8: 4 to 15.
6. John, 15:2.
7. Raphael Simon, O.C.S.O., *Hammer and Fire* (New York: P. J. Kenedy, 1959), p. 238.

CHAPTER V CARMEL

1. On May 1, 1887, M. Martin suffered his first paralytic stroke. He recovered from it and regained the use of his legs, but after Thérèse's entrance into the convent he was afflicted with a series of paralytic attacks and cerebral lesions. His illness, which has been diagnosed as cerebral arterio-sclerosis, was accompanied by paralysis, loss of memory, delirium, obsession, and finally a complete loss of his mental powers. He was well enough to attend Thérèse's investiture ceremony at the Carmel on January 10, 1889, but shortly after that he was sent to a nursing home at Caen where he remained for three years. For the last two years of his life he was brought to Evreux where, broken in mind

and body, he was cared for by Céline in a house lent to her by her uncle. Thérèse, immured behind the cloister walls, received regular bulletins from her family about her father's state but she had no direct contact with him during the last years of his life. He died on the twenty-ninth of May, 1894.

CHAPTER VI CONSUMMATION

1. Cf. St. John of the Cross, *Spiritual Canticle* (B), Strophe 28.
2. St. John of the Cross, *Living Flame of Love* (B), Strophe 2.
3. St. John of the Cross, *Spiritual Canticle* (B) Strophe 36.
4. Translation from *The Pope Speaks, op. cit.*, p. 213.
5. Luke, 1: 46 to 49.

CHAPTER VII PROPAGANDA

1. André Combes, *Le Probleme de L'Historie d'une Ame* (Paris: Editions Saint-Paul, 1950), p. 125.
2. *L'Histoire d'une Ame* (Lisieux: Office Central de Lisieux, 1924), p. viii.
3. Père François de Sainte-Marie, *op. cit.*, Tome I, p. 78.
4. Philippe de la Trinité, O.C.D., "Actualities Thérèsiennes," *Ephemerides Carmelitcae*, VII (1956), p. 534.
5. Baldomero Jimenez Duque, "Literatura Teresiana," *Revista de Espiritualidad*, no. 69 (Oct.–Dec., 1958), p. 602.
6. All these editions are preserved at the Office Central in Lisieux, and I personally inspected them there.
7. I discovered Canon Dubosq's statement, and those of the Carmelite nuns, in documents preserved in the library of the Discalced Carmelite Fathers at Avon-Fontainbleau. This library, the provincial library for the Paris Province of Carmelites, is a rich mine of information about Carmel in France.
8. This very same point was illustrated by a story Msgr. Vernon Johnson told me a few years ago. He had once asked Pauline if Thérèse was considered a saint even before her death. Pauline replied that she thought Thérèse was an exceptionally gifted soul, but there was no thought about her possible canonization.
9. To support her theory, Goerres quotes some testimony given at the trial for Thérèse's canonization:

Abbé Domin remarked at the trial: "Perhaps somewhat too much zeal was applied to the distribution of
books, pictures and other objects pertaining to Sister
Thérèse. But I do not think these efforts were intended
to manufacture a reputation of sanctity out of nothing.
Her sisters in the Carmel were certainly not indifferent
to the success of their efforts—but I am certain that
they acted with the greatest of intention." (p. 393)

Checking the page of the *Processus* to which Goerres
gives reference (II Summarium, p. 972), we find that the
above statement was indeed made at the trial—except
that there is an error of identification: it was Abbé
Dumaine, not Abbé Domin. Abbé Dumaine's testimony
about Thérèse at the trial was not particularly important;
although, as vicar of Notre Dame in Alençon, he baptized
Thérèse, he had no contact with her after the family
moved to Lisieux in 1877. He was the vicar-general of the
diocese of Séez at the time of the trial and he was con-
versant with the growing cult of Thérèse Martin. It was
in this capacity, undoubtedly, that Goerres uses him as
corroboration for her theory. His statement, as it reads in
Goerres' book, states that he suspects too much zeal was
used by the nuns in propagandizing Thérèse's cause, but
he adds that the nuns really did have a genuine cause to
work with and whatever they did was all done in good
faith. And this is precisely Goerres' theory. However, a
study of the actual text in the *Processus* reveals something quite distressing: Frau Goerres has removed an entire sentence from the middle of Abbé Dumaine's statement with no indication that an excision has been made—
and the deleted sentence is important; in fact, it is
directly opposed to the Goerres thesis. After the second
sentence of the above-cited statement, Abbé Dumaine
said: "Her reputation was spread very normally among

the people; I am convinced, for the strongest reasons, that nothing was done to hide anything which could harm the cause." (*Elle s'est répandue très-normalment dans le peuple; à plus fort raison suis-je convaincu qu'on n'a jamais rien fait pour dissimuler ce qui pourrait nuire à la cause.*)

If Abbé Dumaine's statement is now reread with the inclusion of the omitted sentence, a different meaning emerges. What he actually said was that he was displeased at the Carmelite nuns for their zeal in disseminating books and pious objects relating to Thérèse's cause, but then he adds his qualifying remarks: first, there were no efforts made to manufacture a reputation of sanctity (*Mais je ne crois pas qu'on ait travaillé à créer en sa faveur une renommée de sainteté*); secondly, her reputation developed in a perfectly normal way; thirdly, no attempt was made to hide anything which could possibly be interpreted as unflattering to Thérèse.

Goerres has made an excision in a piece of recorded testimony without supplying the usual identification marks to indicate something has been omitted, and it is considered dubious scholarship, at the very least, to remove some remarks from a piece of testimony and then carefully rework the sentence together so that the unsuspecting reader has no suspicion he is viewing censored evidence.